# EMMAUS ROAD

## CHURCHES MAKING THEIR WAY FORWARD

Also by Donna Sinclair & Christopher White
*Jacob's Blessing:*
*Dreams, Hopes, & Visions for the Church*

and by Donna Sinclair
*A Woman's Book of Days*
*Getting Along: The ABC's of Human Relationships*
*Christian Parenting*

DONNA SINCLAIR &
CHRISTOPHER WHITE

# EMMAUS ROAD

## CHURCHES
## MAKING THEIR WAY
## FORWARD

WOOD LAKE BOOKS

Editor: Michael Schwartzentruber
Design: Margaret Kyle
Proofreading: Dianne Greenslade

Quotations from the Bible in this publication are, unless otherwise indicated, from the *Good News Bible* – Old Testament copyright ©American Bible Society 1976, New Testament copyright ©American Bible Society 1966, 1971, 1976.

National Library of Canada
Cataloguing in Publication Data

Sinclair, Donna, 1943-
   Emmaus Road : churches making their way forward / Donna Sinclair & Christopher White.
   ISBN 1-55145-485-8
   1. Protestant churches – Canada. 2. Church renewal – Canada. I. White, Christopher, 1956- II. Title.
BR115.W6S55 2003    280'.4'0971    C2003-910123-1

At WOOD LAKE BOOKS, we practice what we publish, guided by concern for fairness, justice and equal opportunity in all of our relationships with employees and customers.

Wood Lake Books Inc. is an employee-owned company, committed to caring for the environment and all creation. Wood Lake Books recycles, reuses and composts, and encourages readers to do the same. Resources are printed on recycled paper and more environmentally friendly groundwood papers (newsprint), whenever possible. The trees used are replaced through donations to the Scoutrees for Canada Program. A percentage of all profit is donated to charitable organizations.

We acknowledge the financial support of the Government of Canada, through the Book Publishing Industry Development Program (BPIDP), for our publishing activities.

Printed in Canada

# Dedication

To Jim Sinclair
who has the map for Emmaus


&


To my parents:
my father, Patrick White
and in memory of my mother, Jane,
for starting me on the road.
For my wife Wendy,
for keeping me on the road.

# Contents

# Acknowledgments

My work as a journalist puts me in touch with women and men and children all over the United Church of Canada, and with people from other denominations and faiths. They teach me volumes, and I have put as much of that as I can into this book.

My colleagues at *The Observer* are patient, encouraging, and extremely knowledgeable.

The people (including the leadership) of St. Andrew's United Church in North Bay, Ontario, are a constant source of inspiration and hope.

Terry Dokis, with his gentle affirmation of our last book, helped me believe this one could be written.

Wanda Wallace, Kathy Aylett, Sarah Tector, Trish Mills, Muriel Duncan, Lynn Murphy, Rose Tekel, Jane Howe, and Elizabeth Frazer cope most often with my writing-induced absence of mind, and they always welcome my return with such grace.

David Sinclair, Joan Sinclair, Andy Sinclair, Eric Robertson, and Tracy Sinclair (and of course, my mother, Margaret Knapp) all seem to believe I can write books, even when the task looks gargantuan to me. Their confidence is contagious.

Dawn Vaneyk generously allows me to draw on her extraordinary creativity in all facets of congregational life.

The staff at Wood Lake Books is enthusiastic and skilled, a safe home for sweat-stained manuscripts.

Christopher White, my co-author, exudes new ideas and excitement about the church with every breath.

I am enormously grateful to all of the above; and especially to Jim Sinclair, who sees wisdom before it is born.

Donna Sinclair

The Emmaus Road is a story about a journey and the writing of this book was a journey in itself.

I want to thank a number of people: first, my spouse, Wendy, who, when I doubted that I could actually write this book and build a new church at the same time, was a constant source of support and encouragement; my girls, Sarah and Elizabeth, who always fill my life with joy and delight as they grow; and my congregation, Westminster United in Whitby, Ontario, for their ongoing vision, courage, endurance, and daring.

I must especially thank my colleagues in ministry: Gail Brimbecom, Margaret Motum, Sandra Bath, board chair Joanne MacPherson, and our building project manager, Hugh Robertson. These people have been part of an incredible team and it is an honor to work with them.

Friends are a gift and I cannot say how deeply I appreciate the friendship of Robert Thaler, his humor, theological depth, and integrity. A thank you also to everyone who so generously responded to my phone calls and e-mails; your input built this book.

Just over five years ago I picked up the phone, called Donna Sinclair, introduced myself, and explained why we should write a book together. I'm still amazed that she has said yes, not once, but twice! It is a pleasure to write with someone both gifted and committed to all that the church can become.

Finally, to our editor, Mike Schwartzentruber, and all the folks at Wood Lake Books, for believing in this project and patiently giving me the time to complete it.

Christopher White

# Introduction

> While they were walking and discussing, Jesus himself
> came near and went with them, but their eyes were kept
> from recognizing him. And he said to them, what are you
> discussing…? Cleopas answered… "Jesus of Nazareth,
> who was a prophet mighty in deed and word before all
> the people and how our chief priests and leaders handed
> him over to be condemned to death and crucified him.
> But we had hoped that he was the one to redeem Israel."
>
> Luke 24:15–21

W

"e had hoped." Is there any phrase more poignant? So much of human life seems wrapped up in that phrase. It is through hope we persevere; through our stubborn belief that our world can be transformed by the grace of God.

We wrote *Jacob's Blessing: Dreams, Hopes, & Visions for the Church* while the church was struggling with a systemic decline, catalogued by people like University of Lethbridge sociologist Reginald Bibby. It was hemorrhaging members and seemed to be viewed in the wider society with a disinterest verging on hostility.

The churches' response to this loss took two different forms. One approach held that decline was an unfortunate symptom of a post-Christian era. The wheat was being separated from the chaff; a faithful remnant would be left, similar to the first-century community of Jesus' followers.

The second solution was mega-churches, with massive physical plants, high technology production values, seeker sensitive services, and thousands of worshippers.

The problem with the former was its confusion about what faithfulness actually meant. How was it possible that a God of life would want God's church to wither away? There were unpleasant practical consequences as well: declining revenues crippled much-needed programs, and a chasm widened between the national and congregational expressions of our faith. Decline also accelerated the church's irrelevance in the eyes of the wider society; our voices became quieter. Half-empty churches and vacant nurseries simply caused an ache in the hearts of local congregations.

But solutions from the mega-church movement proved equally unsatisfactory. What worked in these massive edifices couldn't be transplanted into smaller congregations with different cultures and contexts. And in a world grappling with ambiguity, the simplicity that was part of the allure of "seeker" services came increasingly into question.

The Emmaus Road story speaks as metaphor to these problems. Like the two disciples, Christian congregations are burdened by grief. Like them, we see our world changing around us. From the collapse of corporate giants like Enron, to the tragedy of September 11, 2001, and the ongoing conflict in the Middle East, we live in a period of corrosive uncertainty.

There are so many questions: What is the role of the church in this new world? What are the implications for worship, adult Christian education, programs with youth and young adults? How will this church speak to its neighbors who share different faiths? What sort of churches should we be building? What should happen within their walls? What sort of leaders do we need?

*Emmaus Road: Churches Making Their Way Forward* is a collection of answers to those questions, often from our own congregations.

[White is a minister in southern Ontario, and Sinclair a layperson in northern Ontario.] We have seen communities of faith recognize the risen Christ in their midst and outside their walls. In many ways, this book is about leadership: the minister as congregational leader and the congregation as civic leader.

Perhaps a look back, earlier in Luke's narrative, will help convey what we mean: Jesus has been crucified and his stiffening body placed in the tomb. Three women disciples have gone to anoint him, but have found him gone and shining angels in his place. "Why do you look for the living among the dead?" the dazzling ones inquire.

It is the stuff of murder mysteries, reversed. Usually there is a body, and the task is to find out who did it. Here, we know who did it, but where is the body? Then Luke takes us abruptly to the Emmaus Road, where the mystery is solved. Jesus is alive and well and traveling with friends. The fact that they fail to recognize him is not as odd as it seems. They know their friend is dead; it would be truly bizarre if they suddenly noticed he was the hiker beside them. Even if the stranger looks precisely like Jesus, the laws of nature are clear and fixed. The dead do not walk and have lively conversations.

But they do. The disciples who had been filled with anguish discover life where there is supposed to be death.

What if we are like Cleopas and the unnamed one (perhaps a woman) who simply do not realize that the Spirit of God remains with us, in our congregations?

What if we are in the early stages of a religious and social reawakening that will be as significant as the progressive era of the early 20th century? What if we gave up searching for that silver bullet of instant success – what Bibby calls "magic potions" – and embraced a new diversity, recognizing that there is no one answer for every congregation?

What if – like the disciples – we stopped focusing on what we have lost, and recognized the strength we have?

Even as this is written, for instance, 300 people from Westminster United in Whitby, Ontario, White's congregation, have signed letters to provincial and federal politicians underlining their commitment to our besieged Medicare. People from St. Andrew's in North Bay, Ontario, join others from the local peace alliance at a vigil outside their MP's office, every Wednesday evening, week after week.

We believe that our congregations are waking up to the discovery that they have far more power for good than they realize. During the churches' period of searching, something wonderful and unexpected was happening. Local congregations were simply rolling up their sleeves and getting to work. Some were amalgamating, some closing, others re-visioning and retooling, while still others began building for the future.

The results of this are, if not spectacular, reassuring. As Bibby discovered during his research for *Restless Gods*, mainline churches have stopped their slide: while 30% of congregations were declining, 30% were stable and 30% were actually growing![1]

When the reality of rural depopulation is factored in, the results are even more impressive. Equally significant is the increase in the United and Anglican churches of those under the age of 35.[2]

This new dynamic came as much of surprise to Bibby as to anyone else. He attributes it to the churches' resilience:

> Simply put, well-established religious groups can be expected to go down only so far before they bottom out. They may be at low points for a while. But as new people with new ideas take on positions of influence, and as human and financial resources are put in place, these companies can be expected to stir, and, to varying degrees, begin to rise again. It's not a question of if; it's a question of when."[3]

We would also attribute this to the recurring reality of the Emmaus Road experience: when you think it is all over, that is exactly the moment when God starts something new. Perhaps congregations are like Jesus, the Christ – full of God, but unrecognized by the world.

Perhaps what we need are the qualities of character of those disciples on that road: their trust, hospitality, welcome.

Take hospitality, for example: Cleopas and the unnamed one meet a stranger (this Jesus) walking along the road, and are pleased to have him walk with them. When he would go on alone, on a road that might sprout robbers at any moment, they prevail upon him to stay with them.

Or vulnerability: the two disciples tell Jesus the deepest things on their hearts. Their friend had been crucified, and they "had hoped that he was the one to redeem Israel."

They were attentive, eager, curious, humble. They drank in Jesus' version of history and politics. What if we were as connected to our own hearts and as creative in our imagining as the two disciples were? "Were not our hearts burning within us," they said, looking back on an encounter that had touched them like flame.

And what if, finally, like them, we were alert to the critical moment. "Stay with us," they said immediately. Not later, not watching him go down the road wishing they had done something. And when, at last, they sat down – that lovely, intimate, human act of placing themselves around a common table – he broke the bread. And they saw him for who he really was.

None of this could have happened without their perseverance and courage, their hospitality, their alertness. This is what the church needs now. If we are to recognize the ones we walk beside, we must look, not to instant solutions, but to our strength of character.

In the chapters that follow, we will try to illustrate some ways to do that.

The story of the two disciples meeting Jesus on the Emmaus Road can help us, as churches, to move forward. It contains all the elements we need – the healing power of community, the nurture of study, the gift of sacrament, the power of outreach, the many gifts of leadership. We invite you to this journey.

# The Inventive Congregation
# Facing the World's Complexity

That same hour they got up and returned to Jerusalem;
and they found the eleven and their companions gathered
together. They were saying, "The Lord is risen indeed"

Luke 24:33–34

**Christopher White**

**Ingenuity:**    clever or inventive skill or imagination.
**Perseverance:** persisting in adhering to a course of action,
a belief, or a purpose; steadfastness.

Charles Dickens, in one of the most famous opening sentences in all literature, wrote that, "It was the best of times, it was the worst of times..." In the first decade of the 21st century, that holds true more then ever before. In his book *The Ingenuity Gap*, author Thomas Homer Dixon suggests that the world is spinning out of control and that our capacity to adapt is being outstripped by the complexity of our world's growing problems:

As the rich get richer in developed countries, average household consumption in Africa has plummeted 20% over the last twenty-five years. In India an estimated 60% of all newborns are in such poor condition from malnutrition, low birth weight and other causes that they would immediately be placed in intensive care were they born in California. Never in human history have we seen such differentials between rich and poor. And these differentials are the main cause of huge and often disruptive migrations of people around the world in search of a better life.[1]

Controversial Danish academic Bjorn Lomberg, on the other hand, takes the opposite approach.

The fact is as we have seen, that this civilization has over the last 400 years brought fantastic and continued progress…We have more leisure time, greater security and fewer accidents, more education, more amenities, higher incomes, fewer starving, more food and a healthier and a longer life…the proportion of people starving has fallen dramatically from 35% to 18% and by the year 2010 this share will probably have fallen to 12%.[2]

Lomberg acknowledges that we face real problems, but he believes that they are solvable and that the world is in reality progressing.

So which of them is right?

I believe that they are both right. Over the last century, through global wars and Holocaust, humanity has shown its capacity to destroy with an evil glee. Yet at the same time, life has gotten significantly better in many ways across the planet. We are living longer and healthier lives, and we produce more than enough food to feed the world – the problem lies in our economic distribution.

The world is filled with dualities, divisions, contradictions, and elements that unify us.

So what does this all mean for the church?

Like the world, it is the best and the worst of times for the church. In North America, the church faces significant challenges. We are in competition not so much with each other, but with a secular society. Sundays have been designated as "charity day." All secular charitable runs and walks are scheduled to conflict with church. Children's extracurricular hockey, skating, part-time jobs, soccer, softball, drama, and even piano lessons, often occur on Sunday mornings. Church is disappearing from the minds of many.

Yet we are told ad nauseam that our society has a deep spiritual hunger. The implication, then, is that if your church is not full the problem is yours; you are not meeting the needs of a society hungry for God.

It is time to question seriously this mantra, which has unintentionally created a consumer mindset in the wider church: congregants become customers whose needs we are to meet with proper marketing and technology. Instead of seeing church as a relationship of mutuality and servanthood, we have reduced ourselves to the language and values of our culture.

Mark Devries, pastor and author of *Family-Based Youth Ministry*, told me that, "People in our society are not hungry for God; they are hungry for angels. Angels don't require you to do anything; they draw no moral lines; they are just there to help." Mark believes that many people have never made a connection with organized religion. As a result, our wider society is skeptical and even suspicious of churches.

Church, in my experience, is hard. It requires courage, the ability to live with conflict, and the ability to make long-term commitments – to not flee when things get difficult. It's like the perseverance the two disciples discovered when they began to talk with the stranger.

Much to their surprise, starting with the story of Moses and moving through the prophets, he conducted a midrash of scripture leading up to their time and their own experience with Jesus.

They walked, they talked, and day slowly passed into evening. Before they realized it, they were in Emmaus.

As they moved down the familiar path towards the comfort of their home, the two disciples felt an emotion they had never again expected to feel: an inner peace that lit up their hearts, though they knew not why.

The stranger passed their door and moved on as though he were going to disappear into the twilight. Urgency filled them and they entreated him to rest, to stay with them, "because it is almost evening and the day is now nearly over."

And so they welcomed him into their home, lit the oil lamps and put together a simple meal to assuage their hunger. The family gathered around the table and they asked their guest to say the blessing.

He lifted the bread, blessed and broke it, and gave it to them. During this sacramental act, they realized that they were in the presence of the risen Christ. And then he vanished from their sight.

Excited, they jumped up, talking to their assembled family: "Were not our hearts burning within us while he was talking to us on the road, while he was opening the scriptures to us?"

We in the mainline church have made a terrible mistake in surrendering to the values of society. When a teenager takes a part-time job that requires working Sunday mornings, do we ever talk to that teen and his or her family to offer our personal and congregational support? Do we help them approach management to ask that they respect our Christian Sabbath, and not schedule his or her shift on Sunday mornings? Do we say, "Stay with us…"? Or do we sadly shake our heads and say, "What a shame. We'll miss having you around."

Where has our faith gone? *Instead of adapting to the times, should we not use the power of the gospel to transform the times for the people who worship with us?* That's what happened with Cleopas and the other disciple.

I have witnessed changed lives in my congregation. I have seen folks with newborn triplets come to church every single week. I have watched blended families with toddlers and teenagers charge through the doors on Sunday mornings, just as the first hymn begins. I have watched people grow as they mentor the homeless into new ways of being, and seen the church positively affect the lives of those who share its life.

Currently, my congregation, Westminster United, in Whitby, Ontario, is in the middle of constructing a new church facility, an enormous task that has taken an unbelievable number of volunteer hours. For some members, it has turned into a part-time (or full-time) occupation. Arranging the financing, dealing with the lawyers, raising funds, coordinating volunteers, and working with the architect and builders – the experience is both exhilarating and exhausting. Yet these people do it because of their faith, because they believe in the value of our shared ministry, and because their lives are enriched not by what they keep, but by what they give away.

Like us today, the disciples on the road to Emmaus were emotionally exhausted, drained, and even frightened. After their encounter with the risen Christ, they found new reserves of strength they did not know they possessed. Immediately, they went back to Jerusalem, the scene of their greatest loss, to embrace the good news, and to live through their pain and find a whole new way of being.

It is that encounter with both the risen Christ and the risen community that is the key to the decades to come. Is the community genuine? Is this a place where I can find authentic relationships and worship that speaks to my heart and head? Is there a place for me, no matter what my age and stage? Is it going to be worth investing the limited time I have in this church? These are the issues we need to address.

## Discipleship

From the late 1980s through the 1990s, many churches placed their hope in the paradigm of the "seeker." The paradigm for the early part of this century will be the disciple. The day of the seeker service as *the* approach for thriving churches is over. In communities such as Freedomize, in Toronto, Ontario, a new ethic is taking its place. Slow growth, high commitment.

If you wish to attend these churches, you are more than welcome. If you wish to become a member, you need to apply. That's correct – *apply*. At Freedomize, people wanting to become members are invited to take a 13-week new members course and must then write a letter explaining why they want to be a part of the church. Todd Cantelon, the 28-year-old senior pastor at Freedomize, says, "we're not countercultural, we are anti-cultural." Long sermons and two-hour services are the norm. On the Sunday night I attended their service, I was the oldest person in a church that was filled with young adults. While I may not personally advocate an application process, these churches eliminate any sense of the "consumer as king" in their approach.

Is it possible that we have failed our people by woefully underestimating their capacity for commitment?

Church writer Robert Webber, the originator of the Ancient Future movement, told me that seeker-sensitive worship services and the megachurches they birthed may have a difficult future. "Mega-churches are the empty tombs of tomorrow. They are boomer driven and will not meet the needs of the emerging generation." For Webber, the future lies in smaller congregations.

Brian McLaren is the pastor of Cedar Ridge Community Church, in Spencerville, Maryland, and the author of *The Church on the Other*

*Side: Doing Ministry in the Postmodern Matrix.* He believes that the future may be more complex. He says,

> I hope that there will be plenty of mega-churches in the future, as well as house churches, virtual churches, country churches, urban churches, high and low and middle churches, denominational and nondenominational churches, traditional and non-traditional churches…I like what Rick Warren said, himself a mega-church leader: "Bigger is not better and smaller is not better. Better is better.[3]

Writer Leonard Sweet puts it well when he says,

> Ministry in a postmodern pluralistic world must bring together the opposites; it must embrace and bridge a world that is homeless and well-housed, a world that is both dying and healthy, a world that is obese and anorexic at the same time. We must reach a world in which economic health and social health seem to be in inverse proportion. The higher our income the worse we feel.[4]

All of these people are correct, even though they seem to both complement and contradict one another. For that is the Zeitgeist of our age – conflict and conciliation, parallel opposites living in a dynamic and constant tension.

In the years ahead, there will be no time to rest on our laurels; we will be constantly reinventing and re-imagining ourselves and our ministries. What works one year will not necessarily work the next. The immediate future (five to ten years) will be marked by the type of diversity that McLaren speaks of, only it will often happen within one church!

One local church may in one month's time and through various venues through the week offer for its congregation's spiritual enrichment the following: a Quaker style meditation service, a Brethren-style communion service, a healing service from charismatic Episcopalians, weekend seeker services à la Willow Creek, a silent retreat with fasting at a Benedictine monastery , a lecture series comparing Calvin's Institutes and Aquinas's *Summa* and more…[5]

In this McLaren is absolutely correct. There will, I believe, be an increasing diversity in the types of worship experiences we offer: Taizé music, jazz, praise, and the traditional all within one service, with smaller specialized services offered once a month or more often to suit other needs. So, too, in Christian education, Sunday school, youth and young adult programming: choice and continual innovation will be the rule.

The church's identity may no longer primarily be found in Sunday morning worship. Rather, its sense of self will evolve and enlarge as it becomes a center for spiritual growth, outreach, and development of mind, body, and spirit.

Last spring I was waiting for the results of my youngest daughter's most recent cardiology tests. I was standing on the fourth floor of the hospital's atrium looking down to the street, where an old woman stopped and emptied a bag of bird food. Immediately, almost 40 pigeons began a frantic feeding frenzy. She then moved a few steps away and emptied another bag containing exactly the same food. The pigeons went mad and flocked to the new supply, even though there was lots of food left in the first pile. Their anxiety was palpable. The scene struck me as a parable to the contemporary church. We seek, in Reginald Bibby's words, "magic potions" to solve our challenges. We dash off to the next big thing, whether it be seeker services or postmodernism, not realizing that we have food for the journey right in front of us.

Yet there is also significant good news. People *are* returning to church; people *are* seeking a foundation for their lives; and, in spite of all the other options in front of them, people *are* committing their time and resources to their church and to God. There is a change in the air, especially when one looks at the global situation of Christianity.

## The global picture

Much to my surprise, it turns out that Christianity is the fastest growing religion in the world.[6] It is exploding across Africa, Latin America, Asia, and parts of the South Pacific. It will continue to be the world's largest and fastest growing religion well into this century and possibly beyond. Churches are springing up everywhere, especially in those countries where the social infrastructure is limited or disappearing all together. The Christian faith appeals to the poorest of the world's poor, and in this it appears that the first century and the 21st century will have a great deal in common.

We are in the midst of one of the greatest expansions of the Christian faith in history, yet the churches of North America act as though nothing extraordinary is happening. Theological pundits write about how Christianity must change or die, but to quote Philip Jenkins,

This kind of liberalism looks distinctly dated. It would not be easy to convince a congregation in Seoul or Nairobi that Christianity is dying, when their main concern is building a worship facility big enough for the 10,000 or 20,000 members they have gained over the past few years. And these new converts are mostly teenagers and young adults, very few with white hair. Nor can these churches be easily told that, in order to reach a mass audience, they must bring their message more into accord with (Western) secular orthodoxies.[7]

For those of us in the North American mainline, this story is almost incomprehensible. We have been so conditioned by our culture to believe that we are part of a declining and increasingly irrelevant faith that at times we appear to believe the secular media more than the gospel, or the evidence before our own eyes. And when we read Bibby's book on our own growth, we are skeptical. But something is happening; the Spirit of God is at work around the world.

To understand the current context of our churches, we can no longer look only into a North American mirror; we need to look globally, for the emerging churches of the world are going to have an impact upon our local context, possibly in ways we cannot yet even imagine. Jenkins believes that the situation is such that by 2050 the phrase "North American Christian" may sound to the ears of the world like the phrase "Swedish Buddhist" does now – a curious oxymoron.

I do not share Jenkins' view, but I *do* believe that our current and future contexts will be shaped by world forces of which we are not yet fully cognizant, and that we are going to have deal with a global church that is by and large evangelical, charismatic, and socially conservative. As Herbert O' Driscoll puts it, "the tides of Pentecostalism are lapping up against the shores of all our churches."[8]

This means that the North American mainline church will need to carefully position itself and its message to be heard in the midst of an evangelical and charismatic Christianity that will continue to dominate the landscape for decades to come.

Our opportunity in the midst of this religious matrix is to understand both the strengths and the weaknesses of the liberal mainline church, to utilize them with a sense of service and humility, and to add a distinctive and unique voice to the world.

Yet if our context is global it is also national and local. What then is the specific context facing us?

## A postmodern context?

Perhaps the most critical area of the North American context lies in the cultural shift from modernity to postmodernism – a term guaranteed to illicit confusion and doubt for many.

For Brian McLaren, this shift is very real. He believes that postmodernism contains five core values that differentiate it from the modern world.

1) Postmodernism is skeptical of certainty. It critiques not only the objective world and other people, but also the self and the self's very ability to know and understand.

2) Postmodernism is sensitive to context. Something can seem unquestionably true to people in a certain time period, or in a certain social group. But those same beliefs can seem silly and laughable to people in other contexts. Knowing is not an individual matter but a group experience.

3) Postmodernism leans towards the humorous. We shouldn't take ourselves or anybody too seriously. Wryness is the posture of postmodernism.

4) Postmodernism values subjective experience. For postmoderns, it's better to simply experience experience than to turn it into another theory or universalize it and proclaim it as Truth.

5) For postmoderns, togetherness is a rare, precious and elusive experience. It is this yearning for togetherness that inspires the oft-heard postmodern motifs of pluralism and tolerance. In a world where everyone sees everything differently, where everyone lives according to different theories, it is far better to practice tolerance and appreciate diversity than to capsize the boat.[9]

McLaren also believes that postmodernism receives unfair criticism as a result of two predominant myths attached to it, the first being that postmoderns reject absolute truth. This, says McLaren, is false; what they reject is absolute knowledge. Equally it is said that postmoderns don't *care* about truth, that they are only concerned with experience. Instead, says McLaren, "If by 'truth' we mean honesty, authenticity, and genuineness, all but the most radical will sign on as believers in a heartbeat."[10]

While I have enormous respect for the work of McLaren and others of the postmodern movement, my instincts suggest that postmodernism is a transition period, one that may well last for the next decade, but is not in and of itself a defining motif for this century let alone the next 500 years.

I find myself in sympathy with the British writer Gilbert Adair, who stated that,

> Postmodernism is, almost by definition, a transitional cusp of social, cultural, economic and ideological history when modernism's high minded principles and preoccupations have ceased to function, but before they have been replaced with a totally new system of values. It represents a moment of suspension before the batteries are recharged for the new millennium, an acknowledgement that preceding the future is a strange and hybrid interregnum that might be called the last gasp of the past.[11]

This strikes me as an accurate description of our times – we are in transition and constant change, moving toward an unclear destination.

## The current meta-narrative: Entertainment Tonight

While it is true that our society currently lacks a *religious* meta-narrative (an overall story, either written or "lived," that we share in common), we *do* share a meta-narrative of a different sort.

As journalist Vinay Menon put it in an article that appeared in *The Toronto Star*,

> From Toronto to Tokyo to Sydney to London to Cairo, from Bollywood to Hollywood and all points in between – never before has entertainment drawn such a sprawling audience. In the future when anthropologists study the last 100 years, they may refer to it as the Entertainment Era, a time when distraction and diversion reigned supreme.[12]

Spending on entertainment shot up by 40% between 1982 and 1999, a time when real incomes increased by only 4%. Events admissions jumped 47%, video games and their equipment 73%, cable TV 253%. As strategic futurist Joyce Gioia puts it,

> Western society was once predicated upon shared values. It was once culturally homogeneous. But then came massive unprecedented waves of immigration, followed by rapid globalization and the rise of mass communications. And suddenly in diverse cities such as Toronto, pop culture became the touchstone and a bridge linking strangers.[13]

Gioia further states that "pop culture has become a religion for some," which, given the reality that 20% of North Americans do not belong to any religion, shores up my belief that entertainment has become the new meta-narrative for our society. From *Survivor* to *American Idol* to the latest hit movie, pop culture has become the only glue and shared value we have in common. I have even experienced this at church. One of the most heated arguments I have ever had was not over worship, theology, or finances, but over the Steven Spielberg movie *Artificial Intelligence*. I considered it a horrible film that was grim, awful, and without any redeeming value. My congregant believed the absolute opposite. She saw *A.I.* as metaphor, a film filled with hope and Christian symbols. Our discussion became quite heated and others who had seen the film chimed in. (It made our later discussions on the shape and worship styles to be used in our new sanctuary quite tame by comparison!) Of course, in retrospect, I realize that what we were engaged in was really theological reflection. The current culture that is so easy to dismiss is also a place where the holy can touch the secular.

A preoccupation with sports is another area where we share some commonality. After Canada won the gold medal in men's hockey at the 2002 Winter Olympics, the nation's streets were filled with dancing and cheering people. Our family got into the car and drove around Whitby. The streets were packed with people honking horns, waving flags, and hugging and cheering each other. It was our medal, our collective victory. We even had a sacred relic à la the Middle Ages to commemorate the event. A Canadian dollar coin was buried at center ice, where the puck is dropped, by the Canadian who was responsible for maintaining the ice during the Olympics. It was removed after the gold medal game and placed in the Hockey Hall of Fame, where thousands flocked to touch it, hoping that good luck would rub off from it as if from the remains of some fabled saint. Lest you think I am being too dismissive, I confess that I too made the pilgrimage. Had we lost the game, the national mood would have been depressed for weeks.

Politics, sex, and religion may not be subjects for polite conversation, but the movie or game you just saw on the weekend is what binds the workplace and the neighborhood together. As pop idols and sports stars become the icons of society, their lives and deaths help shape our values and context. What they eat, drink, wear, and do, become the touchstones around our needs. And when they die, whole nations are transfixed with projected grief. When Diana, Princess of Wales, was killed in a car accident, the whole Western world behaved as though a close family member had died tragically. We grieved because through the media we felt we knew her – and inside we believed *she* knew us.

The power of television defines our tragedies, our griefs, and our delights. Tens of thousands of people die every year in wars that span our globe. Parts of Africa are experiencing a war as wrenching and bloody as World War I was to Europe. Yet it remains invisible to us; we do not see its images on our nightly news, or its pictures on our television, so it does not exist.

If entertainment is now our meta-narrative, it will prove to be only a temporary binding force. The reality is that media and entertainment are becoming more diverse and perverse, programming for increasingly segmented sections of our population. As Richard Worzel says in the *Toronto Star* article mentioned above, "When you talk about entertainment in the future, you will see a much more diverse, a much broader range of possibilities…society is becoming much more fragmented and the implications are that we are going to have less and less in common with those around us."[14]

As the article goes on to say, instead of one global village there will be thousands.

## Worship space at the movies

Even so, this model of entertainment has impacted our churches and our worship. Over the course of my recent sabbatical, I spent time visiting other churches. I specifically went to churches outside of my tradition. I wanted to experience a different view of the gospel from my own and also to experience what it is like for folks when they walk into a church for the first time. It was an enlightening experience on a number of fronts.

One of the things that struck me as I walked into these worship spaces was how dark they were. They had little if any natural light, and what small windows there were, were covered. I found this puzzling. We in Canada get little enough light, especially during the winter months, so why would they not want to maximize their exposure? The answer is simple really; natural light is the enemy of screens and projectors. These churches have bought into the entertainment model of worship. The construction of their sanctuaries has been determined by the needs of the current technology. The argument, of course, is that this makes their worship "culturally relevant." But when we speak of cultural relevance, we need to ask "Whose culture?" We live in a multiplicity of cultures, both demographic and ethnic, so the issue of what is culturally relevant really depends upon who you are and where you sit. Furthermore, the important issue is not so much about worship being culturally relevant as it is about worship being culturally *transformative*. Of course we need to use the tools of our technology and church worship *does* arise out of a particular context. But the gospel is primarily about transformation and creating a different view of the world than that of the current culture. If our current culture is defined by *Survivor* and *American Idol*, the church stands in a very different place with a very different set of values.

## The future today

If our context is beyond postmodernism, then where exactly are we? In Kennon Callahan's most recent book, *The Future That Has Come*, he posits six major paradigm shifts that have affected the church.

1) We think, plan, and live as a movement and not as an institution. We share the motivations of compassion, community, and hope, more than challenge, reasonability, and commitment.

2) We encourage people to make sense of life in this universe and on this planet rather than ignore the discoveries of the universe we are making.

3) We help people grow by presenting them with a balance of excellent "sprinter" and solid "marathon runner" possibilities. ("Marathon" people are willing to make long-term commitments; they will come out to choir practice every Thursday night forever. "Sprinter" people are unwilling to make long-term commitments. They will commit to a four-week Bible study, but not a six-month one.)

4) We encourage people to participate in mission projects that are direct, generous, just enough, and grassroots rather than indirect, conserving, too much, and top down.

5) We help people discover their best creativity and development of objectives for which they have ownership rather than controlling and directing what they should do.

6) We encourage people to discover and live the whole of life, not just an inside-the-church life.[15]

These shifts describe the same phenomena that McLaren and Sweet define as the shift to postmodernism. So what, then, is happening? Are we declining in the midst of a postmodern Methodist-like revival, or something else altogether?

## A new meta-narrative

People need a story upon which to build their lives. As I have tried to show, the power of the current meta-narrative based on entertainment is eroding. In the midst of this, it is clear to me that the mainline church is also entering a new phase in its life. The worst may be past and our future is potentially filled with unique possibilities. We may grow, or we may simply stabilize. A lot has to do with how we respond to a world that is experiencing overwhelming and constant change.

People today face tremendous stress. We are working harder and longer than ever before. Families are under great strain as they try to juggle all the balls they have in the air. September 11, 2001, added a new level of uncertainty about the safety of our societies and a fear of what will happen next. The vicious sniper attacks in late 2002 created a wide sense of unease and dread; no one was safe anywhere. As I write, war with Iraq looms, just as North Korea has announced it has nuclear weapons. Yet the church is called to be a community of safety, a place where fears can be eased and where we can learn how to cope with this uncertain and violent world.

Clearly, as in every other epoch, the church faces significant challenges. Yet this is also a time of great hope – hope for the mainline church to discover its ministry as a bridge between different faiths, denominations, and the secular world. Often, we are attacked for accepting ambiguity, but it is our ability to live in the tension of ambiguity in a world that clamors for clarity that could in fact not only be our greatest strength, but model a new way of being that can save our planet. We have a vital message and the ability to dialogue, to teach, and yes, to preach.

A great Canadian diplomat and prime minister, Lester Pearson, saw this day arriving a half century ago when he wrote that we were moving into a time when

> different civilizations will have to learn to live side by side in peaceful interchange, learning from each other, studying each other's history and ideals and art and culture, mutually enriching each other's lives. The alternative in this overcrowded little world, is misunderstanding, tension, clash and catastrophe.[16]

It is time for the mainline church to re-energize and re-engage with a world that may not always welcome us, but that needs our imagination and willingness to examine alternative ways of being.

This is the new meta-narrative that is in its earliest stages of formation, a religious worldview that encompasses and affirms both the diversity of different faiths and their unity. If we hold on to a belief that one faith alone is true to God and all others must conform to this, then we will explode. Our world needs a new story, one that contains both truth and doubt, certainty and questions – a story that has God at its heart. That is the story, the bridge, that we can help to build.

We offer not security, but a place to embrace ambiguity and, through that action, the opportunity to discover a new way forward. As it was for the Emmaus Road disciples, the best for us is yet to come.

# 2

# The Vigilant Congregation
# Walking When We Cannot See

Stay with us, because it is almost evening and the day is
now nearly over...He took bread, blessed and broke it,
and gave it to them. Then their eyes were opened...

Luke 24:29–31

**Donna Sinclair**

**Alert:** vigilant and attentive; watchful. Mentally agile, responsive
and perceptive; quick.

Picture the two disciples watching the stranger walk ahead, continuing on the road, while they enter Emmaus and the comfort of a known bed. He is just a stranger, someone they don't know, but it could be dangerous for him. It's getting dark and robbers abound.

Of course, perhaps *he* is a robber. Perhaps he only made friends with them so that he could murder them in their beds later on. What should they do?

They don't stop to consult each other or dither. They simply trust their instincts. Luke doesn't distinguish which one spoke, but has them say, almost comically, in chorus, "Stay with us, because it is almost evening and the day is now nearly over."

The quality shown here – alertness – is one we need. It's a kind of hypervigilance to the possibility of the moment when it appears, an attunement to the overarching vision of the gospel, while understanding that that goal is reached in small, human, almost insignificant ways. It is enacted by congregations through gestures we almost don't notice, gestures that occur by instinct out of hearts that are in the right place, and out of already informed minds.

When people have done their homework, they know their role – keep the stranger, the child, and Creation itself, safe – and they are able to act reflexively, the way ambulance attendants and emergency room physicians act. For instance, when the government panel on nuclear waste comes to town on short notice, they know who among them can speak with expertise on the issue.

Discernment is crucial. If congregational members and leaders have been studying the psalms, and have the biblical delight in creation already running in their veins, it's not so hard to know what to say when it's time to speak out on nuclear disposal or other contentious issues.

In congregational work, the moment is everything.

## An attitude of readiness

On September 11, 2001, the World Trade Center in New York City was destroyed. Only a short distance away, the staff at the Seaman's Church Institute, a longstanding ministry of the Episcopal Church, watched in helpless horror from their windows.

But they didn't remain helpless for long. The first thing they did was pray. Then they got busy distributing flyers for the rescue workers, letting them know they had food and showers. Soon, people began to stream in. For the next few months, they fed about 500 workers a day. When the electricity went out, they burned paschal candles for light and cooked firemen's meals on barbecues. They coordinated an endless stream of volunteers.

Six months later, a little group of church journalists gathered in the sun-drenched library of the institute, listening with tear-filled eyes as the staff told their stories – like the one about the man who came to deliver more candles. Because he had a truck, he was pressed into service mopping out St. Paul's Chapel, right next door to Ground Zero. Someone saw him and asked if he would mind cleaning out the nearby Burger King where firemen and police streaming in and out had left a floor deep in ash and mud. Next he was sent to the morgue, just a storefront emblazoned with the spray-painted letters "MORGUE." He willingly mopped that out too, even though he had just come to deliver candles.

Then there was the story of the young volunteer who had come from a great distance, determined to serve. He was only one of many so he didn't get a lot of attention. But he kept asking what he could do. Finally, Debra Wagner of the institute said, "We need hot dog buns." He left silently. An hour later, he was back with 300 of them. "Give that man a name tag," Wagner said.

When they paused between stories, the Seaman's Institute staff explained how they had done this. (And this is what congregations can learn.)

First, they had prayed. Then, they figured out their assets. They had, in addition to showers and a small cafeteria, several priceless re-sources: first, the ability to make photocopies and laminated photo identity cards; second, cell phones; and third, clerical collars, which proved especially important.

This last item gave them access to Ground Zero at a time when those working in unimaginable hell needed to be held and to ask why God had allowed this to happen. The collars made it possible for them to be there to offer last rites to what, in many cases, was a body part, a piece of human flesh.

The people at the institute told these stories humbly and patiently. There wasn't an ounce of egotism or pride in what they had to say. But there *was* a kind of confidence. What they had to offer as Christians, as church, had been sufficient. They had done what Christians do; they had prayed, fed, held, and comforted body and soul. Like the two disciples on the Emmaus Road, they had turned to the stranger and said, "Stay with us."

That same gentle confidence was also found at St. Paul's Chapel, at Ground Zero. Six months after September 11, it, too, continued its strange new ministry. To that same group of journalists, it looked like this: Firemen are sleeping on the pews. A massage therapist is set up in one of the side aisles, and its most historic artifact – the enclosed box that was George Washington's pew – is proudly serving as the podiatrist's workplace, where the omnipresent ash is washed from the battered feet of workers. Every square inch of wall space is covered with drawings and messages of hope, often from children. Directly at nose level, if you are lying down, is one note in a child's careful hand: "I hope you have a good sleep."

The chapel's parishioners, staffmember Sister Grace tells us, are no longer in pinstriped suits and neckties. They are dressed in Kevlar and they wear respirators. "A terrible tragedy happened," she says. "It happened in our backyard. Our congregation coped."

This may seem like a hopelessly specific story, the aftermath of September 11. But it's not. Congregations cope with tragedy all the time. When children are hungry – an ongoing crisis so prevalent many of us are dulled to it – they open food banks. When detainees are threatened with deportation, congregations all over this country open their doors and invoke the tradition of sanctuary.

They are vigilant to the care of the stranger, like those two disciples on the Emmaus Road.

## Walking together as a congregation

Part of the power of the Emmaus Road story also lies in its universal application to the human condition. We walk with others and do not see who they really are. It is true in marriages and in workplaces, in families and in congregations. But nowhere is it more true for Canadians (and for many in the United States as well) than in our relationship with the original people of this land. We walk beside each other and we do not see.

When one denomination – the United Church of Canada – made its apology to First Nations congregations in 1986, almost 20 years ago, it asked them, in the words of the moderator, Right Rev. Robert Smith, "to forgive us and to walk together with us in the spirit of Christ so that our peoples may be blessed and God's creation healed."

But how do congregations do that – not only with First Nations peoples (although that is perhaps the most pressing need) – but with other groups that often seem hidden from our eyes? The key is to be ready.

The following is a story from St. Andrew's in North Bay, Ontario, a medium-sized congregation in a downtown church in a small northern city. The Nipissing First Nation, where the Union of Ontario Indians has their main headquarters, is close to the city. The Indian Friendship Centre is only a few blocks from the church building.

But none of this means that there is a great deal of back-and-forth with the reserve. Instead, there are links. Chippewa High School has always had First Nations students from all over the north, for example. Many non-Native people have leased land and built homes on part of the nearby reserve. And there are mixed marriages. Still, there seems to be an invisible barrier between city and First Nation.

As the eyes of Christians were slowly opened to the sin of the residential schools, the call to cross that barrier seemed more insistent. But how?

It was a long, slow, imperfect, but creative process. It began about 25 years ago (before the residential schools had burst onto national consciousness) with a quiet, long-standing friendship – the kind often enjoyed despite the barrier – between one congregational member and the head of the Indian Friendship Centre. There was trust between two people.

Then, a Timmins dentist and church member, David Humphrey, decided to donate his fine and much-loved collection of First Nations art to Manitou Conference. The collection had expanded beyond the walls of his home; he wanted it to be in places where people were constantly coming and going, and would be touched by it as he was. Each congregation received one or two pieces of art.

St. Andrew's promptly displayed the two they had received in the most-used rooms, the chapel and the sanctuary. The paintings were visibly cherished.

Later, when the conference sponsored an exchange with South African churches, in the days before apartheid ended, they invited a Native elder to come along. He, in turn, was always willing to speak at local events. St. Andrew's invited him often. In fact, the congregation was always alert to a Native presence who might offer wisdom. When they heard an elder from Moosonee was coming to town, he was invited to take the pulpit that Sunday morning. When the denominational headquarters had a guest visiting from the Mayan Presbytery in Guatemala, he was invited to town, and the pulpit.

The congregation was vigilant for any chance to learn from and honor Native wisdom, an almost reflexive response to opportunity.

Then the Friendship Centre was closed for renovations. A request to use the church parlor for some meetings was met with a yes. The large painting by artist Bebaminojmat, a work that spoke profoundly of Nativity and new life, was moved to the parlor to welcome them. Soon, some afternoons, the scent of ceremonial sweetgrass drifted through the hallways and into the sanctuary at St. Andrews.

Meanwhile, the congregation was struggling with the usual issues faced by a downtown congregation, in an area with significant out-migration of its young people. The participants in the small group called United Church Women were getting older and less able to carry on with the teas and bake sales that they had done so graciously. So the congregation invited the second chief from the Teme-Augama First Nation, Rita O'Sullivan, to spend a day with these women talking about the role of the elder in her culture.

Her words offered the women a new identity and a new task. As feeding and serving the congregation became less their responsibility, the dignified role of carrier of wisdom and memory became larger.

At the same time, First Nations people and non-First Nations people alike were using the food bank and Jobnet, two ministries of the congregation that were marked by their dedication to treating those who came to it with respect and care.

And the labyrinth was brought to St. Andrew's – along with the drum – by an Ojibway elder, Terry Dokis, the same Nipissing professor who had gone to South Africa with Manitou people. He was not a United Church person, but he treated the church with respect.

By now, some First Nations members of the congregation were beginning to claim their heritage, and the simple fact of their presence and manner was beginning to affect St. Andrew's. The extraordinary attunement to the earth-as-mother that is foundational to First Nations experience began appearing as an element in prayers. A Lenten retreat found stations in the sanctuary representing the four directions and the elements, earth, air, fire, and water.

A women's retreat focused on prayer and braiding sweetgrass, with questions flowing freely, and hands busy, touching the hair of mother earth. Ideas and hopes flowed back and forth, too, in an atmosphere of respect.

None of this means that the walls between two cultures have been destroyed. Perhaps they shouldn't be. The dominant culture could still overwhelm with good intentions. But there are gates in those walls and people pass through them with more ease than before.

There is also recognition of the holy between us. The strangers we once were to each other are no longer, and there are glimpses of the divine instead.

None of this happened by accident, although there was no grand design. It happened without much formal statement of intent, except that the congregation is in a Conference that has said First Nations concerns are paramount. Mainly, the walls were breached because the church leadership remained constantly alert for every opportunity to soak up wisdom from First Nations culture, and the whole congregation quickly responded to that vision.

If this story was found in an institutional or corporate setting, it might be referred to as an example of "emotional intelligence," leadership that is highly skilled in relationship. Rutgers University researcher Daniel Goleman (who invented the term) says that, "by acting from a place of emotional intelligence, and modeling that behavior, leaders can help their employees embrace an ideal vision for the group."[1]

This ideal vision cannot be forced. At St. Andrew's, it took 25 years. "The process of slowing down and bringing people into the conversation about their systems and their culture is…critical," says Goleman and his colleagues.

The congregation had time to attune themselves to First Nations art, to listen to elders, to hear the wisdom for themselves. They didn't start by discussing hunting or fishing rights, or land rights, or other possibly contentious issues. But when tough issues like the Oka crisis – more than two months of armed standoff between Mohawks and the Canadian army, near Montreal – came along in 1990, they were well-equipped to support their denomination's efforts to be in solidarity with First Nations people there.

## Conclusion

Like the disciples on the road, like *all* disciples on the road, we cannot see what lies ahead. Often, we do not see clearly who walks beside us. But we can learn from the disciples to trust our instincts. We can set in place the attitude of care and compassion that informs those instincts. The two disciples, after all, had been taught by Jesus himself to care for the stranger. The staff at the Seaman's Institute, with whom we began this chapter, functioned out of a long history of care for the marginalized. When the moment of extreme crisis came, they could trust their intuition to help them react wisely.

Congregations can do that. And, in so doing, we may recognize the Christ.

**3**

# The Comprehending Congregation
## Listening to Others

> When he was at table with them, he took bread, blessed
> and broke it, and gave it to them. Then their eyes were
> opened and they recognized him; and he vanished from
> their sight. They said to each other, "Were not our hearts
> burning within us, while he was talking to us on the road,
> while he was opening scriptures to us?"
>
> Luke 24:30–32

**Christopher White**

Generosity:      showing a tendency to recognize the positive
aspects of someone or something.
Liberal, broad; favoring the recipient's interests
rather than the giver's.

Understanding:   the ability to reason and comprehend, harmony
in opinion or feeling, a sympathetic perception,
awareness, or tolerance.

This passage contains the heart of the Emmaus story. It is *here*
that recognition occurs. It is here that the truth the disciples
knew all along, but dared not believe, is opened to them,

through the sharing of a meal, the simple elements of bread and wine that bind us all together, no matter our race or creed. It is in that meal that truth is experienced and heretofore unimagined possibilities are opened up before us.

We are at a point in the life of the church when we are being called to imagine radically new ways of being that have been barely dreamed of, let alone put into practice. As I argued in Chapter 1, this possibility is the beginning of a new religious meta-narrative for an emerging world.

Historically, North America was bound together by the Judeo-Christian narrative. The Christian story formed, by and large, the subtext of our society. We said the Lord's Prayer in the schools. School Christmas concerts featured re-enactments of the birth story of Jesus. Yet as our society became more diverse and increasingly secular, this binding narrative began to unravel. In its place grew the secular story of consumerism.

Religion, and not just the Christian religion, disappeared from our schools and became a rarer part of media content. Instead of attempting to add different faith experiences to the common culture, faith was effectively removed from the public square. It was set at the margins of societal discourse, seen as a purely private matter. Further, religion became something to be feared. Dave Stephens, journalist and host of CBC radio's *Ontario Today* put it well when he told me that because journalists are afraid of appearing to put one faith over another, they simply choose not to include *any* faith discussion around the issues of the day. As a result, to the media, religion has become little more than a mix of curious cultural festivals, that may make a good 30-second visual for the nightly news, but that has no place in the heart of society.

This misunderstanding of what religion is effectively ghettoizes faith and fails to address the reality that for millions of North Americans, and for billions of people around this planet, faith shapes their worldview. The tenets of their religion help people to discern how they react to society-wide issues, from politics to culture. But in the public square they are silenced. The situation for millions of people is like that of a fish pretending there is no water.

The churches have been unsure how to react in response to this rapid change. Some became defensive; others created their own media outlets to share their perspectives. For a time, we were almost apologizing for our very existence.

But all that has changed. A newfound confidence, stripped of both pretense and arrogance, seems to be the current posture of the mainline churches. Once again, we are owning the positive contribution that faith can play in society. We are reinvigorating our worship, seeing it not as a sideline, but as the event out of which our outreach, education, and common life comes. For millennia, our faith traditions have had ethics as a core value. Now, once again, we are both speaking and acting out on issues from health care to social justice to corporate responsibility.

Yet how do we frame issues of ethics and faith in an interfaith context? How do we create a common, shared understanding of the good?

To even engage the task will require dialogue not only *between* faiths, but *within* faiths. As Philip Jenkins points out, one of the challenges for the mainline churches is going to be their need not simply to converse with fellow liberals of other faiths, but with Pentecostal and other evangelical Christian churches in other parts of the world. We need to do this not only for our society, but for the future of our civilization.[1]

How are we to enter into this dialogue and what are the blocks that stand in our way?

Every writer has a bias. A church writer, for example, has a theological perspective that informs his or her perspective. Perhaps it is best, then, that I start by sharing my own bias, my own perspective.

For me, Jesus is the center of the Christian story. His resurrection is a reality that is more than wishful thinking, or an idea that somehow evolved over time. It was the event that changed everything. Equally, I do not see Jesus as a wisdom teacher, cynic, or traveling magician, but as one so infused with God that the incarnation becomes real in him. Through Jesus, God becomes personal; God shares our life and death. Without Jesus, how can God understand my pain, my grief, my joys and celebrations? In Jesus, God becomes particular and individual, the Word become flesh.

## Our way may not be their way

So far so good. A problem arises, however, if I try to take those beliefs to another level and cram Jesus and God into a restrictive box that claims that unless you believe as I do, you cannot be saved. Judgment and anger can transform the gift of belief into a curse. For me, the Christian faith is my reality, but it is not one I can impose on anyone else, because their perception of the reality of the divine may be very different from mine.

My own view of the diversity of the world's religions is this: God loves us. The whole story of the Bible tells of God's yearning to be in relationship with us. As a parent loves each child in a unique way, God's love for us is shown in the multiplicity of faith expressions in our world. Each religion is God saying, "I love you." As with each child in a family, our love grows in a unique way that reflects our personality and life. So too, God's love is shown in our differing faith traditions.

The problem is that throughout history religions have sadly reacted like the spoiled child who proclaims, "Mom loves me best." It's not true. Each child is loved and they need to remember that so too are their brothers and sisters.

## Reductionist bargaining is not the answer

The other challenge to genuine progress and understanding is the tendency to see interfaith dialogue as reductionist bargaining. I'll give up Jesus as the Son of God if you give up your belief in the Torah as complete revelation. This, as Bruce Feiler points out in his book *Abraham: A Journey to the Heart of Three Faiths*, leads to an artificial dialogue that has, "tried to gloss over variances and produce manifestoes of shared ideals. This effort often yields bland paeans to loving one's neighbor, not murdering people, and striving toward the universal Oneness of the Good Life Universal."[2]

While I am strongly in favor of everyone loving their neighbor and not killing each other, I agree completely that we have missed the real point of the exercise. The goal is neither to impose my faith on someone else, nor to reduce the core tenets of my faith in a misguided attempt to make it palatable to others.

## The dignity of difference

God loves diversity; God loves difference. Modernity attempts to eliminate difference because it interprets it as threat. It sees the claims of the great world religions as mutually exclusive and contradictory. They *are* contradictory, that is the point, but it is humans who see them as mutually exclusive, not God.

What Feiler and a host of others advocate is a different kind of conversation – one that does not minimize differences, but rather accentuates them; one that does not ignore the variations among the routes to God, but stresses that even the idea of other routes is acceptable.[3] This goal is not to eliminate the differences, but to learn to respect them.

Feiler's words and work are echoed even more strongly by Dr. Jonathan Sacks, chief rabbi of the United Hebrew Congregations of Great Britain and the Commonwealth, in his book *The Dignity of*

*Difference: How to Avoid the Clash of Civilizations.* This, in my view, is quite simply the most important book of the new millennium. It has caused Dr. Sacks great grief in that he has been the target of strident and extremely hostile reactions from his Orthodox rabbinic colleagues. He has been accused of heresy and told that his book should not be in Jewish homes. As Sacks is Orthodox himself, this has been a source of tremendous pain for him, only somewhat mitigated by the support he has received from his Reform and Conservative colleagues.

So what has Sacks written that has caused such an outcry? Simply this:

> I believe globalization is summoning the world's great faiths to a supreme challenge, one that we have been able to avoid in the past, but can do so no longer. Can we find, in the human other, a trace of the Divine Other? Can we recognize God's image in one who is not in my image… Can I, a Jew, hear the echoes of God's voice in that of a Hindu or Sikh or Christian or Muslim… Can I do so and not feel diminished but enlarged?[4]

Religion, he believes, is far more central to our collective future than we have been led to believe. Whereas politics moves pieces on a chessboard, religion changes lives. Sacks understands and affirms that faith "builds communities, shapes lives and tells the stories that explain ourselves to ourselves."[5]

Sacks' whole argument rests on the proposition that our differences as faith communities can be a source of real strength for us and our planet. He challenges the notion that sameness and universality are the ultimate good by showing how the biblical narrative values difference.

> God, the creator of humanity, having made a covenant with all humanity, then turns to one people and commands it to be different, *in order to teach humanity the dignity of difference.*

Biblical monotheism is not the idea that there is one God, therefore one truth, one faith, one way of life. On the contrary it is that *unity creates diversity...* God creates difference; therefore it is in one who is different that we meet God. We encounter God in the face of the stranger [italics mine].[6]

Is this not the core of the Emmaus Road story? It is the stranger who is the bearer of hope; the stranger who walks with the disciples through their grief and comforts them; the stranger who challenges them and shakes them out of their lethargy, and who reawakens their imagination. It is in the face of the stranger that they realize there are no true strangers, but only glimpses of the God, whom even death could not conquer.

George Lindbeck, a Christian professor at Yale, is the founder of what has been termed the "postliberal" school of theological thought. In an article entitled "Answering Pilate: Truth and the Postliberal Church," William Willimon defines Lindbeck's theology not as

a description of some universally available experience, but rather an expression of the faith held by a particular religious community... A Jew and Christian differ not in using a different language to describe the same experiences of God, but in having learned different languages and listened to different stories, which have given them different experiences of God.[7]

Willimon goes on to say that, "from a Christian point of view, we must care for the distinctiveness of our language and the distinctiveness of our community formed by that language..."[8] It is the distinctiveness and unique attributes of each faith community that together make the tapestry of God. It is that tapestry rather than a monochromatic blanket that reveals a direction to God.

But the challenges before us are immense.

## Not a stranger, but a friend

She stood at the front of the church on an early November Sunday. The initial shock of September 11 had faded and we, like everyone else, were struggling to make sense of the impossible. A week earlier I had received a call from a civic official inquiring what the churches were doing in response not only to September 11, but to the hostility that was being directed at Muslims in our community. I told him our response and now I watched nervously as Raheel Raza made her way into our pulpit.

Raheel is a writer, speaker, and Muslim layperson who had been recommended to me as an excellent speaker on Islam and the issues of September 11. I would be less than truthful if I did not admit to a certain anxiety on that morning. I didn't know what she was going to say and I didn't know how my congregation was going to react. I didn't know if I would be celebrating or doing damage control after she spoke. The media was present, which heightened my internal tension, but I need not have worried. She was, in a word, magnificent.

Raheel Raza was a gift to our congregation that morning. She entranced our children and gave the gift of her faith to those assembled for worship. She spoke of an Islam we had rarely heard about in the media. She redefined terms such as *jihad* in ways we had not considered. She spoke of peace and condemned without equivocation the terror of September 11 and all terrorist acts. She spoke with courage and conviction. We welcomed a stranger and found a friend.

Since that morning, Raheel has made over 25 similar presentations across southern Ontario. Churches of all denominations have opened their doors to her message and bridges are being built between communities. Raheel has become an apostle of hope and has dedicated much of her life to interfaith relations. What we discovered that morning is that differences enhance God; they do not reduce God.

I have, in my congregation, a family that is originally from Trinidad. The parents were both raised among Christians, Muslims, and Hindus. They went to each other's festivals, holidays, and high holy days. Their Christian faith is rich and profound, as is their respect and complete acceptance of these other paths to God. Their experience has enhanced and enlarged them.

They, I pray, are the future – multifaith families who simply assume that there are alternate and equally valid paths to God, families who see this as a profound gift and never a threat. This is our hope: that our eyes will be opened and we will see God around us, with our hearts burning within us, not in anger, but in joy.

As North America becomes more and more ethnically diverse, we have an opportunity to ensure that our congregations reflect this reality. The question may simply be, how? How do we become truly hospitable to our neighbors? What does respect for diversity really mean for us as congregations? How will that be reflected in our worship and structures? These are critical questions for our future.

Perhaps a place to begin is to start a dialogue with those congregations who rent our spaces. Could we invite them to partake in a shared meal, or a worship experience, or a conversation about our respective traditions, history, beliefs, and core values? This could provide an opening for both churches to learn and grow together.

At Westminster, we are making a new beginning in this direction. In 2003, we are, as Christians and Muslims, holding a dinner together – to share food, to share faith, and to share hope, believing that in the breaking of bread we can discover God. Who knows where it will lead? But it is a beginning.

## One church, separated by a common language

Perhaps our greatest challenge is to find ways not only to talk *interfaith*, but to rekindle a dialogue with evangelical Christians. This will prove extremely difficult as there is much suspicion and unhappy history on both sides.

It is easier for liberal mainline people to talk to liberal Jews and Muslims than to speak with evangelical Christians. If you go into our respective bookstores, it is as though you are dealing with different faiths as opposed to different branches of the same faith. We have profound differences on a range of complex social issues. We each have stereotyped the other. We each suspect that the other does not really know the Bible. The mainline church suspects the evangelical church of rejecting academic rigor and of using the Bible as a literal proof text. Evangelicals fear that liberals see the Bible as only a vague, watery guideline, the equivalent of Aesop's fables. We distrust their certainty; they distrust our comfort with ambiguity.

Brian Stiller, president of Tyndale seminary, told me that during his tenure as head of the Evangelical Fellowship of Canada he received more hurt, more lack of courtesy, and more distrust from United Church clergy than from anyone else. On the other hand, a colleague of mine tells of going to an evangelical church to listen and to learn, only to be told that God was not with him because he was United Church. There are enough brickbats to toss at both sides for a millennium.

Brian McLaren believes that a new dialogue needs to happen and suspects that will begin between postliberals and postevangelicals.

This dialogue has already begun. In the book *The Nature of Confession: Evangelicals & Postliberals in Conversation*, a series of essays outlines how bridges can be built. Theology professor Philip Kenneson defines postliberal Christianity as

> not primarily either a set of propositions to be believed or a
> set of inner experiences to be expressed. Rather, the Christian

faith is viewed as the medium in which one moves, a set of skills that one employs in living one's life. Postliberalism does not encourage believers to find their stories in the Bible, but rather they make the story of the Bible their story. It is the text, so to speak, which absorbs the world, rather then the world the text.[9]

In other words it is belonging before believing.

By seeing the Bible as the story around which we form our lives and communities, a dialogue can proceed. It would be tragic if we can not find common cause with members of our wider church, at the same time as we find common cause with those of other faiths. The dignity of difference means embracing the challenge of living with those with whom we do not agree. That is sometimes easier to do with the stranger than with your estranged brother or sister.

One final point. In order for us to dialogue, we need to understand our history and, I would argue, our doctrine. Rev. Dr. Karen Hamilton, General Secretary of the Canadian Council of Churches, told our congregation that it is the concept of the Trinity that will be the most challenging aspect of our conversations. I would only add that the Trinity, with its dynamic tension and mystery, is one doctrine we need to embrace and revitalize. The future, I believe, lies in a rediscovered and revitalized understanding of the three persons of God. The Trinity is the living embodiment of God's unity and diversity. It is the divine dignity of difference.

# 4

# The Prophetic Congregation
## Walking with the Outcast

...Jesus of Nazareth, who was a prophet mighty in
deed and word before God and all the people, and how
our chief priests and leaders handed him over to be
condemned to death...
Luke 24:19–20

## Donna Sinclair

**Prophet:** a person gifted with profound moral insight and
exceptional powers of expression.
**Courage:** the state or quality of mind or spirit that enables one
to face danger, fear, or uncertainty with confidence and
resolution.

Prophets always make me cry. That sounds like a country song,
but the tears are a touchstone (although an embarrassing one)
telling me when I am in the presence of one with "profound
moral insight" and the courage to express it. Some images of prophecy
that make my heart overflow:

In *Fury for the Sound*, for example – a documentary by filmmaker
Shelley Wine about people trying to save the ancient trees of British

Columbia's Clayoquot Sound – one elderly white-haired woman, wearing a T-shirt declaring "My Canada includes Clayoquot Sound," shakily but proudly reads a prepared statement to police officers before she is taken to jail: "I accept with great pride the honor of being arrested," she says, "and standing on guard for Canada, as my great-great-grandfather did."

Another example: turning on the television news to see my then 21-year-old daughter, Tracy, being interviewed. She is wearing an orange vest with ARC-Observer on it, explaining how the Royal Canadian Mounted Police at Burnt Church, New Brunswick, had rammed the First Nations fishing boat on which she was a church-sponsored human rights observer. Earlier in the newscast, the police denied capsizing the boat. But she looks straight at the camera and explains how she was there, in that boat, and then in the water, and how the police had rammed them not once but twice, throwing all four people (one of whom couldn't swim) into the ocean. Then they pulled them out and arrested them.

## Consequences of speaking out

Both these stories indicate the important question raised by resistance. If we take these examples seriously, as part of the gospel journey – Jesus the prophet, on the cross; the women at Clayoquot Sound; and human rights observers everywhere – are we willing to accept the consequences? Will prophetic activity split the congregation?

Prophets are resisters of the status quo in which most of us are securely embedded. In general, we are as happy to be disturbed as a sun-drenched rattlesnake stepped on by an unwary hiker.

I believe that's part of why I start the waterworks whenever I meet a prophet. I am not brave and I can see the cost coming. Every church member is not going to agree to a joint action, or even whether the particular circumstance that provokes it is a problem. Witness any demonstration for social justice, from the Winnipeg General Strike in 1919, to anti-poverty activists arrested at Queen's Park in Toronto 80 years later.

Second, prophets can become predictable. Poverty, environmental issues, peace crises – the issues that provoke them don't go away easily. It's a rare gift to be able to speak at church meetings again and again, without those present shifting uncomfortably in anticipation of words they will hear as hectoring or scolding.

Third, a congregational leader, or a whole congregation afire with social issues, can be consumed itself. How do the prophets among us keep going? How does a congregation that is constantly at the center of things keep from burning itself, or its leaders, out? How does it keep the conflict prophecy always arouses at a manageable level, without having too many members leave in a rage? It's hard to fight for justice and lead a congregation at the same time, as minister, or as active layperson on an outreach or education committee.

These are not easy questions. But we cannot avoid them. In fact, simply existing as a community of faith in a secular society is a subversive act: "Feed my lambs," said Jesus. Some feel the lambs should hustle out and find a job, even if there are none they can do. While the story of the Emmaus Road teaches us that Christ lives on, the only way we will see him is if we have the courage and intuition to invite him, the prophet "mighty in deed and word before God and all the people," to stay.

Some leaders have found a way to resist the world's wisdom and to go straight to God's. They plunge with passion into reshaping the world, still keeping wonderfully diverse congregations together.

Perhaps it is because they understand the following.

## Prophets need people

Even Jesus did not attempt to do his healing work without his disciples around him. This means that congregational leaders who envision their congregation as a positive force for change must find ways to bring a large part of the congregation onside, without alienating those who cannot join them. It requires a peculiar combination of openness and respect, affirmation and challenge. During a great debate about gay ordination, in many congregations there were forums and study groups, which allowed anyone with strong feelings – which was pretty well everyone – to raise their voices.

In the congregation I attend, like countless others, people were listened to with care. Nobody asked them to think the same way as the leadership (and the minister had made his position clear), just to listen in return. Some people were so appalled by the notion of treating a gay or lesbian person as respectfully as anyone else that they left. Not many though. And those who did make the move to another, less liberal church, were later visited by the minister – a blessing on their right to decide for themselves where they stood on one of the great prophetic issues of the day.

For a long time, the status quo in religious circles was that to be homosexual was to be a second-class citizen, not free to consider the ministry as a vocation, not free to have their union with another gay person ceremonially blessed within their congregation. Those strictures were lifted only by collective action. Those who are gay or lesbian willingly brought on board straight, often uncomprehending people. They needed each other, and the affirmation brought by the other, to have the strength to continue.

The same was true at Clayoquot Sound, and at Burnt Church, and continues to be true today at hundreds of other places where ordinary people declare the presence of wrongdoing. They are surrounded and sustained by others who feel as passionately as they do.

## Prophets are self-differentiated

The fact that prophets are sustained by others doesn't mean that they don't speak with their own voice. Sustained by others, but also self-sustained and self-defined, they stubbornly speak their own truth. Let me illustrate, from my daughter's experience at Burnt Church. Tracy was arrested, handcuffed, and taken by boat and car to jail in Shippagan, New Brunswick. Later, she recalled on paper the following conversation.

The officer said to me, "You know, the Natives aren't too fond of the RCMP." From there we were told that they hadn't been aware that there was only one cell, and they couldn't have a man and woman in the same cell so I would be taken to Tracadie, where there was a cell with a woman in it. Shane would be left in Shippagan.

I told them I didn't want to go. I remembered Pierre had warned me that they'd try to make one feel alone. The officer said that he would get in shit if he let us both be in the same cell. I told him I really did not want to go because I didn't want to leave Shane by himself; he was more vulnerable that way. The RCMP told me that Shane was an adult and could take care of himself.

While Shane was in the calling room the other police officer took down my height, eye color and weight. I asked if I could get my camera back but he said no. I said, "Don't you need a warrant?" He said, "It has been seized as evidence." I got in the cop car and we headed on our way to Tracadie…

Then the cop asked me questions like, "Are you being paid for doing this?" and we started having a big discussion as to whether or not the Natives should be fishing. He talked about lobster conservation and regulation of fishing. He asked me if there were a lot of kids on the reserve. I said I wasn't sure and he said that there was not going to be enough lobster for their kids. This dispute continued and I told him that the real problem wasn't the Natives' fishing, but the large commercial fisheries who fish deep and get the big lobsters. And I told him that fall was the Natives' traditional fishing time and they throw back the soft ones and the females with eggs. I asked him why white people should get all the fish/lobster and I asked him how he would feel if, because he was French, he wasn't allowed to do things that were part of his French identity.

The dispute stopped eventually.[1]

The prophetic aspect of the latter discussion lies in the fact it took place at all. Tracy was aware that isolation itself could silence her observer's role. She chose to continue that role, to bear witness to the justice of the First Nations position on fishing rights. Her self-definition as human rights observer demanded that she retain the ability to think and speak from her own values, even under her new and rather powerful definition as detained person.

Shifting to the congregation, this is what church leaders, clergy, or active members or entire congregations do. They lead. They remain themselves. They function out of their own values, despite all efforts to force a new definition of leader upon them. They have a vision, derived from the gospel, and they follow it while staying connected to the people around them.

## Continually and humbly pray

All of this means that prophets must find ways to support those values. Prayer is crucial. Any person – or any congregation – involved in prophetic justice is tempted at times to let the huge work consume them. The pause to talk to God seems too much time to take out of an overfull life; and the intangibility of prayer in the midst of concrete needs makes it seem expendable.

Indeed, as Roman Catholic priest and author Henri Nouwen found two decades ago in Latin America, some Christians believe that too-heavy a reliance on certain kinds of prayer just diverts them from the work. In *Gracias: A Latin American Journal,* he describes a meeting in Lima, Peru, with wonderful young men and women who are working with the poor. He encountered some among them, though, who dismissed the prayer of charismatic groups as "not Christian prayer since it does not come from or lead to the *lucha* (struggle) for the liberation of God's people."

That, says Nouwen, denies "the need of many people to find a still point in their lives where they can listen to the voice of God in the midst of a sad and war-ridden world." [2]

For many of us in North America, that necessary "still point" of prayer is found in the seemingly mindless task of weeding the garden, walking the dog, or sitting quietly in church on Sunday, waiting for church to begin.

It is also found in whatever allows us to talk with God individually or together – the prayer that begins and ends each committee and board meeting, prayer circles that meet regularly, prayers at the bedside of those who are ill.

And it is found in the prayers for Sunday worship. There is something marvelous about the layperson walking to the front of the sanctuary clutching the paper on which they have written the prayers of the people. Some (myself included) find this terrifying, and their voices shake. Sometimes they manage more sermon than prayer, more preaching than intercession. But always there is a moment – perhaps naming the ones who are in hospital – when the rest of the congregation knows they are overhearing a conversation between a Christian and their God.

That miraculous sense of presence is crucial to those who would do any kind of justice work in, with, or from their congregation. Nouwen says he "has the feeling that those who want to be active in the struggle for freedom for a lifetime will need an increasingly strong and personal experience of the presence of the Spirit of God in their lives."[3]

## Resist the world by the way you are, as much as by what you say

I see it almost every Sunday. Just as the hurry-back-to-the-garden (that includes me) crowd is rushing out of the building after worship, a young couple, say, or an older single person, is coming in. Even though our congregation tolerates remarkable informality in dress and manner Sunday mornings, they will be subtly different.

They will look a little uneasy. They won't know anyone. They will not be well-dressed.

And then someone – often the minister – sees them and greets them with pleasure, and often by their name: "Come on upstairs. How are you? Have you had a good week?"

Our ministers have always been able to argue articulately on behalf of the poor. But they never speak so well as when they are simply greeting an impoverished person by name, with compassion, cherishing their dignity as they do. This happens in congregations all over this country. We need to celebrate it.

In the same way, congregations whose members resist societal pressures (especially after September 11, 2001) against refugees, who accompany them to immigration hearings or who offer them sanctuary, are saying volumes about the gospel imperative to hospitality. And they are powerfully resisting the way of the world. In October 2002, for example, Union United in Montreal was sheltering potential deportees to Algeria. As Union's pastor, Rev. Darryl Gray, said to journalists at the time, "There comes a time in a person's, or an institution's life, when we cannot obey a law our conscience tells us is unjust."

Not that every member resists in the same way. Part of maintaining a prophetic congregation is to accept unconditionally whatever gifts of resistance a member can bring. Some of us will never carry a picket or make a speech, but simply by stocking the food bank, with its implicit leaning toward the poor, we are at odds with those who say the vulnerable do not matter.

## Tell stories

The ability to switch channels on television has made tuning out voices a finely honed skill. The voice of the one who always leaps to point out wrongs can be heard as nagging. Wise prophets tell stories instead – about the child who loves the Special Olympics, for example, but who can't take part this year because government cutbacks mean he has no running shoes; or about the pregnant woman who dies under house arrest because those same cutbacks made simultaneously collecting welfare and a student loan an illegal activity.

The rabbis (like Jesus), with their parables and narratives, have it right.

## Stock bookshelves with enlightened theory

A prophet in a comfortable, liberal society is always in danger of being seduced. Resistance – to those who would harm creation, or to those whose highest Lord is their profit margin – can get to be too much trouble. It becomes simpler to hire the lawn care company to look after the church lawn, even though it uses pesticides. Or, in the inevitable prioritizing to decide which causes the congregation can espouse, to choose the easiest ones: the petition for human rights overseas, perhaps, as opposed to fighting a slanted referendum on First Nations land rights here in Canada.

It's wise to have many books – in the church library or in the individual libraries of church members – by authors who ignite your thinking. These kinds of books are massed in such a way on my own bookshelves that one often simply falls to the floor at just the right time. I will stumble over it while looking for something else and (to the detriment of my schedule) find myself soaking up its wisdom.

At a low point recently, I picked up the newspaper to see an account of a speech by Ursula Franklin. The Quaker physicist and retired professor had been speaking at the Ursula Franklin Academy, a public high school in Toronto that bears her name. *Globe and Mail* columnist Michael Valpy had been there, and he quoted the gist of her speech:

> You can't just use justice to promote it just for yourself, or promote peace just for yourself. It must be for all...You can't have justice and peace alone. You must have community as well.[4]

I felt renewed. If you are involved in prophetic work, it means you go around, antennae out, looking to be fed.

## Feeding the prophets

If you are struggling to be a prophetic congregation, you will need the following.

- Study groups. Never underestimate the power of a small group of people armed with books, fact sheets, and videos.
- Bulletin boards, placed in areas where people have to wait or often mill around. Never underestimate the power of the written word when it is approached by those compulsive readers who cannot take a bath without reading the shampoo bottle.
- A church library, stocked with current periodicals as well as with books.

- A regular troop of passionate speakers, not necessarily Christian ones. It is always heartening to discover that the Good News appears in many forms.

## Study the gospel for courage

To be brave, you need the example of the One who seemed afraid of nothing. "Was it not necessary that the Messiah should suffer these things…" Jesus says to the two mourning disciples on the Emmaus Road.

There is great pleasure in studying the life of Jesus closely, in comparing one gospel to another, one translation to another. This means making Bible study readily available.

When we study the gospels in this way, the fact that Jesus was a prophet becomes as inescapable to us as it is to our Muslim kin, who have always called him one. That kind of close look at Jesus also brings him to life in the midst of the congregation. It evokes the vital presence of the one whose "ecstatic vision and social program," in the words of theologian and author John Dominic Crossan, "sought to build a society upward from its grassroots…on principles of religious egalitarianism…" This was "a challenge," launched at "…civilization's eternal inclination to draw lines, invoke boundaries, establish hierarchies and maintain discriminations. It did not invite a political revolution, but envisaged a social one at the imagination's most dangerous depths."[5]

As Crossan points out, the transformation of the heart that Jesus set into motion was terribly dangerous. Following in his way is less risky here and now, but it is still precarious. Protesters against economic globalization are tear-gassed. Human rights observers are dumped from their boats and arrested. People who hug trees end up with a criminal record, not an uncomplicated history in a time when getting a job entails passing a police check.

It is easy for a congregation to embark on "prophetic utterance and lose its nerve," says one minister with a long history of activism. "You need to study scripture to be supported by the foundational element of the gospel."

## Match prophecy word for word with pastoral care

Some of us, by nature, are better at confrontation than at compassion – or at least, we place the emphasis more heavily on the second part of that word. A congregation where a large group of members has a habit of getting into the papers, or where the leadership encourages the subtle listening necessary to hear the wounded, must encourage those listeners to be attentive to those within the congregation who are in pain. Every hour spent on the picket line needs to be matched by an hour spent in the living room of someone who is lonely.

Fortunately, the volunteer pastoral care team can be one of the strongest communities in the church.

## Accept help from those who are prophetic by role

Interns and students enter a congregation armored with the fact that they are learners. They can make profound and terribly helpful "mistakes" that are really prophetic utterances which can change the hearts of the mighty. Then they escape outrage from those who have been offended (and of course, prophets always offend someone, it's their business) by leaving on cue to return to their studies.

In the same way, church leaders whose role is to speak on behalf of the larger church or interfaith groups often provide support with pastoral letters, or their presence.

### Know when to purr, and when to roar

Good leaders are not anxious. A prophet is made calm by the presence
of God within. A congregation that has learned to roll with the punches
does not wring its collective hands. It speaks gently and is well-heard.

There is no power like that of a white-haired grandmother or
great-grandmother at a microphone. Put the elders forward. They were
raised in an age when good manners were expected, and they know how
to speak politely and firmly. And – when it comes to street protests, in
this country at least – most security forces are still embarrassed to arrest
the grandmothers.

But there is also the time to shout. Carol McBride was chief of
the Timiskaming First Nation when Toronto City Council was engaged
in debate about sending the city's garbage to the Adams Mine. That's
an abandoned open-pit mine, now water-filled, not far from where I
live in Northern Ontario. The council wouldn't give her permission to
speak about hazards to the groundwater caused by dumping trainloads
of waste into a lake. So McBride shouted her piece from the visitors'
gallery.

One newspaper called her "shrill." There are times for that. Congregations need their capacity to make noise, along with their courage
and their pastoral care.

All of this is especially true when it comes to cherishing the land,
a particular form of prophecy and resistance today. I am not sure why
so many tree-huggers are women, but I think it may have something to
do with a land that is in terrible pain, and women's traditional role as
the ones who sit with pain. It may have something to do with women's
traditional ability to hear the voices of those who have no words: small
babies, and the inarticulate but suffering farms and forests.

Women's groups in the church could do worse.

## Consider even difficult truths

Once, in a book in which I described my grandmother, I explained how Barney, as we called her, had emigrated from Scotland at age 18, unskilled and alone. She had gone to work as a maid in a big house in Vancouver. I talked about her courage, coming to a place she didn't know, traveling across Canada alone.

I was amazed at the family discussion this innocent little volume produced. "She did not have go to work as a maid," one relative declared. "You have got the story wrong. Momma was a governess, never a servant."

In that revisioning of my own family history, I became fully aware of the power of denial. I had researched stories on widows and single mothers, and had found the same little trick of the human psyche at work. Deny that over 1.2 million children in Canada live below the poverty line. Deny that the poverty rate for lone-parent households headed by women in Canada is higher by far than for any other family configuration. Deny that it could ever affect me.

It wasn't until I faced my own relative's annoyance at the way I told my grandmother's history as an economic refugee from what she always called "the old country," that this really hit home. One reason poverty is so intractable is that we defend ourselves against the knowledge of it.

In all our congregations, we, or some of our friends or parents or grandparents are, or have been, poor. The prophets of the church will refuse to deny the harsh fact of poverty's existence.

## With resistance comes joy

While prophecy is dangerous, few congregations crack over it. Some people may leave, if a congregation persistently and faithfully seeks out and lives the truth. That is sad.

What these people miss, and what the rest of the congregation may glimpse, is the profound joy of recognizing the Spirit within their walls. As Crossan says in his discussion of the disciples on the Emmaus Road, "finally they recognized him when once again he served the meal to them as of old beside the lake. And then, only then, they started back to Jerusalem in high spirits."[6]

We as a Christian church yearn for those high spirits, for those moments when we recognize the Spirit within us and beside us. "The symbolism is obvious," Crossan says about the story, "as is the metaphoric condensation of the first years of Christian thought into one parabolic afternoon. Emmaus never happened. Emmaus always happens."[7]

May Emmaus happen, born out of courage and prayer and study of the gospel, in your congregation.

# 5

# The Caring Congregation
## Looking after Others

That same hour they got up and returned to Jerusalem;
and they found the eleven and their companions gathered
together. They were saying, "The Lord has risen indeed,
and he has appeared to Simon!" Then they told what
had happened on the road, and how he had been made
known to them in the breaking of the bread.

Luke 24:33–35

### Christopher White

**Compassion:** pity, inclining one to be merciful.
**Tenderness:** easily touched or wounded, sensitive to pain or grief,
loving, affectionate, fond.

The essence of Christianity is community. The whole of Jesus'
movement is predicated on the belief that we worship and
live, not as a collection of sovereign individuals, but as a community that is responsible to and for one another. The opening act of
Jesus' ministry was to choose disciples, to choose to be in community.
God, as understood in the Trinity, exists as a dynamic three-person
community.

The disciples Jesus chose were just like you and me – flawed, imperfect people who struggled to understand life and God. Jesus traveled with this group of men and women, who lived together and shared their gifts with one another. They formed a community, an extended family that has been the model of the church ever since.

The church is a family. The problem, as my friend Bob puts it, is not that we don't treat each other as such, but that we *do* treat each other as members of the same family! As I reflect on the dynamics of every family I have ever known, including my own, I understand exactly what he means.

But for all its flaws and challenges, the church community has the capacity to act in ways that are unique to our society. The church, for example, is one of the last voices that can challenge the greatest heresy of our time – the myth of the primacy of the sovereign individual. This myth, supported by media, politicians, and huge corporations, has devalued and reduced us to playing the role of passive consumers. Everything is a commodity to be bought and sold. The "invisible hand of the marketplace," a great mythological figure of our time, will guide us all to prosperity and happiness, albeit with some unfortunate but unavoidable casualties along the way. To the extent that we succumb to this myth, we are stripped of our role as citizens and members of a wider community.

The church of Jesus Christ challenges this myth with a story that is both bold and fresh.

After experiencing the risen Jesus, the Emmaus disciples did not react as soverign individuals, concerned only for their own well-being; they reacted as members of a *community*. It was to the community that they automatically returned, eager to share their incredible news. It was in community that Jesus' resurrection became fully formed and understood. In sharing their individual experiences, they created a collective memory and a deeper understanding of something that was almost beyond comprehension.

Throughout history, the community of faith has worked to achieve not just the difficult, but the seemingly impossible. Jesus taught us, through his example, the power of community. The disciples, as they began the first churches, showed us the power of community.

Today, churches like ours are still showing its effectiveness.

## One faith community in action

It started as a question.

"Jamie,* what's that underneath your arm?" The nine-year-old had just come in from playing with his friends and was changing his shirt, when his father noticed a swelling under his arm.

"Don't know. It's been there since yesterday," came the reply.

Jamie's mother is a nurse. When she got home from work that day, she took one look at the swelling and whisked Jamie to the local emergency room. Twenty-four hours later, he was at Toronto's Hospital For Sick Children, preparing to begin chemotherapy. He had an aggressive form of cancer, with tumors spreading rapidly throughout his body. It was a nightmare for Jamie, his parents, and his entire family.

It was a shock for our church as well. "What can we do to help?" was the question of the moment. What *could* we do in the face of such fear and worry?

We gathered as a community and prayed at a special service. People donated money to offset the costs of food and parking, which always creep up during an extended hospital stay. As the chemotherapy began, it was clear that we were talking *months*, not weeks, of hospitalization. It was then that the community of the church rallied and people began to respond with the type of practical help that makes such a difference in a situation like this.

When your child is in hospital, the whole experience dominates your life. Time and the world pass you by and your only reality is your child, their health, and the small room you both inhabit. Even getting

* *Not his real name.*

out for an hour to eat lunch and breathe fresh air seems an unimaginable luxury. Knowing this from personal experience and working with our parish nurse, we asked members of our church if they would be available to travel into Toronto to sit with Jamie for an hour, so that his parents could get a break at lunchtime.

The response we received was more than we could have hoped for. People came by car and train to sit with him. Some spoke to their employers and explained why they needed extra time at the noon hour, and always received it without complaint. Jamie received visitors who played games and visited with him while his mom and dad took a precious 60-minute break. This went on for months and I lost count of how many games of Crazy Eights I lost to that small, brave soul.

For Jamie, the outcome was positive. The chemotherapy shrank the tumors and today there is no trace of the cancer in his body. Even so, it was a dreadful experience for Jamie and his family – one that will remain with them for a very long time. I know that the time the church community invested in that hospital made their nightmare a little more bearable.

The whole experience was, to me, a testament to the strength and power of our community. The community of faith lives out its mission in moments like these – not in words, but in its collective actions.

Last November, *The United Church Observer*, our national magazine, arrived in my mailbox. Upon opening it I saw some familiar faces and read an article that came as a complete surprise. It was written by Doug Mackay, the father of a set of triplets from our church. When he and Carolyn discovered that they were going to be parents to not one but *three* children, they wondered how on earth they would cope.

Once again, it was the church that provided the emotional and spiritual support they needed. We sat down with them and realized that it was going to be at feeding times that this family needed our support. So we set up feeding teams that came in the morning and at lunchtime. The

20 volunteers came from their homes and on their way to and from work. For nine months, this family, not to mention the volunteers, benefited from the care of our congregation.

Within this same time period, *another* family gave birth to triplets. At one point, we had *two* sets of feeding teams working with the two families.

I know from talking to both families the difference this made in their lives. As Doug himself put it in the *Observer* article,

> To us, church is far more than it was before, the one hour in the week (while the children are in the nursery) that Carolyn and I get to spend together. It may not be the weekly date that many would appreciate; but we are surrounded by love and friendship.[1]

Just today I received a letter from Cornerstone Community Association. Cornerstone is an organization that works with the homeless and the formerly homeless to integrate them into society and to give them real hope. Westminster has been providing volunteers for a mentoring pilot project with the formerly homeless in our city.

Our mentors meet regularly with these men, to provide emotional and practical (nonfinancial) resources to them. Among other things, the program helps to overcome the isolation and loneliness felt by these people who are on the margins of our society. But both parties grow from the mutual sharing of their lives. By entering into a human life, as God through Jesus entered into our lives, we learn a new way of seeing each other.

When Jesus came to the disciples on the Emmaus Road, he changed their lives, not by supernatural special effects, but by the simplest and most profound of human exchanges, a conversation. Conversations can change the world. And conversations are one thing that the church can provide in abundance.

Similar examples of community building like these from Westminster are repeated countless times around the world, in churches like yours and mine.

*This* is the heart of the gospel; this is the way we look after one another. The early church grew in Rome not because of the brilliance of its liturgy, but because of the quality of its *community*. During a plague, when the authorities left the sick to die in the streets, *Christians* were the ones who ministered to and cared for the afflicted. People understood not through the words that they heard but through the actions that they saw that this group of people marched to the beat of a very different drummer than the one who called Romans to the Coliseum. The church grew because of its ability to create communities that made people's lives better. Christianity is a practical faith that creates intentional communities.

## Social capital

This is church at its best. This is the true strength of community, or what Robert Putnam calls "social capital." For Putnam, the term social capital refers to "the connections among individuals – social networks and the norms of reciprocity and trustworthiness that arise from them."[2]

In his seminal book *Bowling Alone: The Collapse and Revival of American Community*, Putnam puts forth the premise that American (and I would argue Canadian) society has had its core bonds loosened. He identifies the loosening of our civic ties and sees it, surprisingly, through the decline of bowling leagues. Putnam shows that we no longer bowl together or go to church together in the same numbers as in the past. Participation in civic organizations, political parties, and even the political process has dropped. Our capacity for social contact, in the form of card-playing with friends and neighbors, or meeting over dinner parties, has declined drastically. Engagement in our larger society has fallen off, with fearful results.

Why is this happening? In part, social changes such as two-income families, commuting, and a generational change, are responsible. But, for Putnam, the worst cause is television.

People who say that TV is their primary form of entertainment volunteer and work on community projects less often, attend fewer dinner parties and fewer club meetings, spend less time visiting friends, entertain less, picnic less, are less interested in politics, give blood less often, write friends less regularly, make fewer long distance phone calls, send fewer greeting cards, and less email, express more road rage than demographically matched people who differ only in saying that TV is not their primary form of entertainment.

Nothing – not low education, not full time work, not long commutes in urban agglomerations, not poverty or financial distress – is more broadly associated with civic disengagement and social disconnection than is dependence on television for entertainment.[3]

Putnam isn't alone in his belief in the negative impact of television. John Locke, in his book *Why We Don't Talk To Each Other Anymore: The Devoicing of Society*, shows how the very technology we love is reducing real community and our capacity to trust one another.

Today trust is in free fall. The percentage of Americans who agreed that most people can be trusted fell by two-fifths between 1960, when 58% did, and 1994, when only 35% were so trusting. At the same time there was a loss of confidence in basic institutions, from banks and businesses to governments and schools.[4]

The culture of television isolates us from one another, reduces interaction, and renders us passive consumers of the culture. Further, this distrust has both a social and economic impact. Francis Fukyama says that "widespread distrust in a society imposes a kind of tax on all forms of economic activity, a tax that high trust societies do not have to pay."[5]

This lack of social engagement can be measured by the impact of television upon societies that have only recently received it.

Rev. Robert Thaler had his first church in Newfoundland. The people in his community talked about how in the past, on Friday and Saturday nights, the whole town would become a traveling party that moved from kitchen to kitchen. Someone would break out a fiddle or a harmonica and impromptu intergenerational dances would start. Then television arrived. The parties stopped and people stayed home to watch TV each weekend.

We need to start the parties again.

## Pew potatoes?

All of this does, I believe, have implications for our worship life. Reginald Bibby's use of the term "magic potions" is instructive here. Are the screens and projectors that churches are turning to today simply another magic potion? If we use these holus-bolus in our worship, are we not, in fact, reinforcing the television culture? Do we turn worship from a truly live event, into an experience for pew potatoes?

I ask these questions as a pastor who uses these media, but who wants to be sure that we are being responsible and not simply accommodating to the dominant culture.

This leads us to the question of cyber communities as opposed to real communities.

## Cyber communities

As I type this, my 14-year-old daughter sits in front of the desktop computer at the other end of my home office. She is on MSN. This messaging service has overtaken the telephone as the primary vehicle for adolescent communication. She has 30 contacts on her list, all people she knows. It is how she stays connected. Connection is very important for her generation. It is not *one* person she wants to talk to, but many, simultaneously. This is not a cyber community, however, but the *real* community of her friends from school, church, ballet, and her extended family. The computer does not *create* a community; it is simply a tool to facilitate community connections. *Real* community is built by real people, in face-to-face interaction with each other. This is something that the secular world is beginning to understand very well indeed.

"Conversation Café" is a new movement that began in Seattle, Washington. It is based on the very simple premise that talking face-to-face is the most effective tool we have to change society. Taking a page from the coffee houses of 18th-century England, the founder of this movement, Vicki Robin, believes that conversations can

increase social intelligence, build social capital and generate social engagement so we can actually have a wise democracy…

I envision a culture of conversation – a culture where people can talk freely – without fear or taboos – with friends and strangers alike… we get our news from the TV, retreat into private subcultures through online chats, and interact with people who see the world as we do. This is a formula for weakening society enough to allow forces of repression to take over. Conversation Cafés are an attempt to reverse this trend.[6]

It appears to be working. Conversation Cafés are springing up all over North America in response to the vacuum created by our contemporary isolationist culture.

The hunger for genuine community is being expressed all over our society. We need the personal; we need the interactive to be person-centered, not technology centered. In Jesus, God became personal. The church can do nothing less.

## New hope?

If connectedness and community are central to the Christian experience, how do we create that within churches?

This is a question that Randy Frazee has struggled with in his congregation. In his book *The Connecting Church*, Frazee notes that there were problems in how his people experienced genuine community in church. For a time, Frazee believed that the small group model was the best way to facilitate the type of community enjoyed by the early church. However, as time went on he began to discover a community deficit in these small groups.

> I identified fifteen characteristics of community, centered around common purpose, common place, and common possessions. When I compared these to what is found in the typical American Christian small group movement, the gaps were glaring.[7]

For Frazee, nothing less than a radical change in the typical living patterns of North Americans is required. He shares the chilling story of 73-year-old Adele Gaboury.

> When her front lawn grew hip high they [the neighbors] had a local boy mow it. When her pipes froze and burst they had the water turned off… the only thing they didn't do was check to see if she was alive.[8]

It turned out that Adele Gaboury had indeed died. But it took four years for the neighbors to discover this. What was left of her was found by the police. The heresy of the myth of the individual prevented even her next-door neighbors from realizing that she was dead.

In our culture, we are so isolated that if the doorbell rings unexpectedly, we perceive it as threat. Someone probably wants to sell us something. Usually, our suspicions prove correct. Our own homes have become the castle keep, our alarm systems the moat.

Frazee wants us to fill in the moat and open the front door to each other. His suggestions are many, and each of them is important.

He believes that we need to re-create neighborhood: to play out front, not in our backyards; to rediscover and rebuild front porches, not back decks; to set a geographic boundary of two kilometers and live as much as possible within that radius; to shop, walk, and send our children to school within that zone; to spend time with our neighbors; to free up our schedules and learn how to play again. But perhaps his greatest challenge to us is to confront consumerism head-on.

One of consumerism's principles is rights over responsibility. In this system, the pursuit and protection of one's rights always wins out over one's responsibility to his or her neighbor... Consumerism seeks to curb the negative feelings of isolation; we spend increasing amounts of money in an attempt to feel better. However, the more we are obsessed about applying consumerism as a solution to our loneliness, the more it feeds the individualism mindset. It's a vicious cycle.[9]

Instead of consumer-driven individualism, Frazee advocates interdependence: knowing and helping others as we are known and helped; sharing meals, responsibilities, and even possessions; going to church regularly; and spending time with friends and families. If there is a more counter-cultural and biblical concept than that, I have yet to discover it.

But how in this insanely busy world we have created do we get there? How do we create this biblical community?

Robert Putnam reminds us that we are not the first generation to face this challenge. In the Gilded Age of the late 19th century, there was widespread cynicism, a celebration of the wealthy robber barons, and a growing gap between the rich and the poor. Yet the Gilded Age ended and was replaced by the Progressive Era, a time when society strengthened the bonds of her citizens and experienced an explosion in the growth of social capital.

> In an extraordinary burst of creativity, in less than a decade (1901–1910) most of the nationwide youth organizations that were to dominate the 20th century were founded: the Boy Scouts and Girl Scouts, Campfire Girls, 4H, Boys Clubs and Girls Clubs, Big Brothers and Big Sisters…playgrounds, civic museums, public parks.[10]

That creativity went on and on and reshaped the content and context of society. It is time, Putnam believes, to begin a new progressive era. In Canada, the Romanow Commission on the future of health care showed how passionately committed Canadians are to the notion of a single-tier, publicly funded health-care system. This, in the face of an unrelenting attack upon it by right-wing media and politicians. Canadians instinctively know the value of not-for-profit public health care, designed around the needs of the citizen, and not driven by the need for profit. We value the *whole* of society, but the fight is far from over.

Yet the tide may be turning, and the churches can be a part of that.

As we create new forms of social capital, it is important to realize that being in community is not easy. It is hard, at times, and it is easier to be distracted by the entertainment culture than to find time for ourselves and others.

Part of the solution may be emerging in the movement back to the ancient church tradition of common practices. These disciplines are being revived in Protestant churches in North America and in Europe. In the United Church, the five education centers spread across Canada have covenanted to share five core principles.

1) Engagement for Justice
2) Attending to the Spirit
3) Dedication to Learning
4) Commitment to Community
5) Retreat

These are lived out, in the words of Five Oaks director Mardi Tindal, through

> daily prayer; reading scripture; receiving and giving support
> for spiritual growth; sustained learning and action for justice
> and discernment about the faithful use of resources such as
> our own bodies, time and money.[11]

All of the five centers are participating in a two-year pilot project aimed at creating genuine Christian community.

As the Ancient Future movement continues to gain ground as an alternative way of being church, we may see more local congregations attempting to live out a common life. The growth of Taizé-style worship and the ongoing interest in labyrinths point us in a direction that is both new and old.

Perhaps, however, we could start simply, with shared meals on a Sunday evening, followed by an intergenerational worship.

We could also

- plan social events – cards, book clubs – or sports nights if you have a gym (rent one if you don't)
- start a theatre group
- turn off the TV for Lent and plan programs at your church instead
- hold a multigenerational prom (Why should the teenagers have all the fun?)

- sponsor a conversation evening, the Christian conversation café, between neighboring churches, synagogues, and mosques
- create partnerships with other agencies that build social capital – Habitat for Humanity or its equivalent
- sponsor refugees
- work with the homeless – ask your community leaders where the holes are in your social fabric and begin a movement to plug them.

Begin with one conversation at a time. And, if in doubt, do what we did three weeks ago. Go bowling. Just not alone.

# 6

# The Hospitable Congregation
## Embracing New Understandings

Are you the only stranger in Jerusalem
who does not know the things that have
taken place there in these days?
Luke 24:18

**Donna Sinclair**

**Hospitality:** cordial and generous reception of or attitude toward
guests.
**Confidence:** trust or faith in a person or thing. A feeling of
assurance, especially in oneself.

This passage reminds me of times when, overwhelmed by the
world's pain, I go on a news fast. Not for long, mind you. I am
too addicted to at least one daily paper, three on weekends, to
sustain my disenchantment. Still, the weight of information that flows
through my door like a semi-melted iceberg is lightened only by my
spouse's equal fascination with news and analysis.

Jim often deals with the news first, and presents it – properly in
context – at coffee time, when anything seems bearable. Sometimes

there's a hint of the disciples' consternation in his voice, though, as he explains. It seems impossible to him that anyone could not "know the things that have taken place there in these days."

Knowing what has taken place is important. It requires careful reading of the events and currents of the day, and careful listening to the comments of those interviewed about them. Above all, it needs careful testing of those comments against the data church people often have available to them – the comments of people on the ground: inner-city workers dealing with poverty; church partners and our own personnel overseas; First Nations people who understand the issues from the inside.

Their understandings can change our worldview. Our own culture is surveyed from the perspective of another's. We become more critical, though not necessarily less loving, of our own country or province, our own class or ethnicity or religion. We simply discover a different place to stand.

Furthermore, pushing our own biases, seeing the world through the eyes of others, emphasizes the sisterhood and brotherhood of us all. Given the stresses on our sense of global family solidarity, that's a gospel understanding – that we are *all* the loved children of God – to be cultivated. The Christian congregation, equally devoted to personal transformation and the mending of the world, is an ideal place for our worldview to be expanded, for our sense of mission to be cherished and tested for faithfulness.

So how do we properly meet the stranger on the road? Cleopas and the other disciple conversed with Jesus, and listened to him interpret "the things that have taken place there" in the light of history and scripture. How do we do that, as congregations? How do we stretch our understanding so that it is broader and richer and more compassionate?

## With true hospitality

Willard and Doreen Davidson were staff associates at St. Andrew's, the congregation that is my home. When they became part of the staff, a subtle change came over the building. The washrooms were painted. A table was set up by the entrance, full of little things a new person arriving would need to get acquainted – bulletins, newsletters. A bouquet of flowers was often added. New signage helped people find their way around the rambling old building. And by their conversation, knowing your name, genuinely seeking after your health and your opinions, the associates made you feel welcome. They (like other staff associates before and after them) were very wise in the ways of hospitality.

Hospitality is a complicated virtue. In author Henri Nouwen's skilled analysis, two things are required: poverty of mind and poverty of heart. "Someone who is filled with ideas, concepts, opinions and convictions cannot be a good host," he says. "There is no inner space to listen, no openness to discover the inner space of the other."[1]

At the same time, says Nouwen,

a good host not only has to be poor in mind, but also poor in heart… when we are able to detach ourselves from making our own limited experience the criterion for our approach to others, we may be able to see that life is greater than our life, history is greater than our history, experience greater than our experience, and God greater than our God.[2]

The way we see God is crucial in this discussion. Christians worship a God who became a child, a "God who spans the heavens, but comes on tiny feet,"[3] in songwriter and musician Ralph Johnston's words. Somehow, if we want our congregations to have a richer and more expansive worldview, we have to enable them to be broad and humble at the same time, like our incarnate God. It is out of that Christ-like vulnerability that they can truly hear the wisdom and feel the yearnings of others.

But how do we create this emptiness, this open inner space? The Davidsons had part of the answer: a reflexive habit of welcome, born out of a genuine love of others; a humility that sent them cheerfully to work cleaning and painting a grungy washroom, and setting out flowers in the hall. Those efforts create a sense of warmth and safety where it's easier to be open.

But it's also helpful to keep human nature in mind. Most of us don't like change as much when it involves grungy and outdated belief structures.

## Clinging to the status quo

Ministers who try to help their congregations be hospitable to new views of the world must always deal with those whose hearts will not be unlocked. As rabbi and family therapist Edwin Friedman explains in *Generation to Generation: Family Process in Church and Synagogue*, resistance to change is a normal human phenomenon; and it's usually just at the moment that the leader is functioning best, and change is moving along with some speed, that the brakes go on.

How to cope with this? A natural reaction on the part of a conscientious leader is to try harder. Not only ministers do this, Friedman points out. Teachers, parents, clergy, and politicians who meet opposition to the changes they contemplate often end up functioning "as if their followers did not know what is good for them, and furthermore would never change if it were not for their efforts."[4]

But the more leaders struggle to persuade the congregation of the wisdom of their point of view, by trying to "push, pull, tug, threaten, convince, arm-twist, charm, entice, cajole," the more some members will resist. "It rarely occurs to people at the top," says Friedman, "that some threshold has been reached..." The pushing and cajoling simply sets people in their ways even more and "further efforts will not only fail to bring change, but will be converted into forces that stabilize the status quo."[5]

Most congregations have seen this process. Many years ago, I watched a young minister preach brilliantly, over and over, against the Vietnam War, to a congregation that would not move one inch into active protest. More recently, while passionate efforts in my own denomination to help congregations become "affirming" to gay people are often successful, they are also sometimes met with equal resistance.

## Confident, connected leadership

The leader must do everything possible, then, to be confident he or she has chosen a faithful path. That involves prayer, seeking out wise advisors, studying the gospel, and looking back over the history of the congregation to understand it better.

The minister should also keep in mind that if some anxiety is appearing, it probably means movement is occurring. That's what is making people ambivalent. Even if some have been yearning for new meaning and action, they may still feel as uncomfortable at the first invitation to sit in with poverty activists as the Hebrews did, when they pleaded with Moses to return to the slavery of Egypt.

When this happens, the leader must stay connected with the congregation. He or she should remember and trust the work they have done to discern this path and vision. Above all, the leader must hold on to her or his own sense of self, remaining self-differentiated.

"If a leader will take primary responsibility for his or her own position as "head" and work to define his or her own goals and self, while staying in touch with the rest of the organism, there is a more than reasonable chance that the rest of the body will follow.

There may be initial resistance, but if the leader can stay in touch with the resisters, the body will usually go along.[6]

Of course, it is hard to do both. Introverted leaders will want to retire to their study and read books, seeking to bolster the vision. Extroverts will want to spend all their time persuading people. The dual process of being "a self while still remaining a part of the system" is difficult, Friedman admits, but it will "convert the dependency that is the source of most sabotage to the leader's favor instead."[7]

A self-differentiated leader will carry on, respectfully helping the congregation broaden their sense of what is possible.

At Trinity United, in New Glasgow, Nova Scotia, for example, the Futures Committee, with then-minister Rev. Norm Marple as a member, set out to bring new life to Sunday worship. They studied, attended a workshop, read books, and tried to fit what they had learned into a vision for their own context. Then they began to experiment with non-traditional approaches to Sunday morning.

> They kept the congregation carefully informed about every prospective change. They made well-rehearsed presentations, figuring out in advance their answers to critical questions. They talked in the service itself about what worship meant. They acknowledged openly that change is painful. But they never backed away from leading, calmly, toward the confident vision they had developed. "The Futures Committee had been appointed to bring about change," says Marple. Given the committee's longstanding mandate, "we did not feel we needed to be given permission."[8]

Another example of sensitive, calm leadership is found in the experience of Sydenham Street United, in Kingston, Ontario, as they became an "affirming congregation," fully welcoming to gays and lesbians. The process of broadening the congregation's collective worldview to fully include people of any orientation was spread over many months.

The volunteer Affirming Congregation Study Group patiently listened to all concerns, even asking members to write letters to them to be sure they were heard clearly. They invited in high-profile speakers, Ontario Human Rights Commissioner, Keith Norton, for example. They held a special service during which gay and lesbian people told their stories. Christmas Eve, after the congregation had been well into the process for several months, was marked by the baptism of the child of a lesbian couple – a service "etched in the memory of the church," says committee member Bruce Hutchinson.

They reported monthly to the church council, keeping the power structure of the congregation fully informed, and drawing on its support.

In short, they did everything possible to stay in touch with the constituency, at the same time as they stuck to the path that they had come to understand – from careful study – to be a faithful one.

Now, explains Hutchinson, services of holy union for homosexual couples are celebrated. Members of the youth group do not tolerate homophobic jokes, and the children of lesbian couples feel at home in the Sunday school. A (gay rights) rainbow symbol is on the church sign; rainbow symbols are on congregational name tags. A rainbow flag – a signal that this is a safe place, whatever your orientation – stands in the sanctuary. And while that flag means one longtime member won't come into the sanctuary, that member did not leave the congregation. Every effort was made to be sensitive to the minority (21%) who voted against the change.

Sometimes, Hutchinson says, a gay person enters the sanctuary for the first time, sees the flag, and begins to cry.

## Conclusion: A checklist for changing worldviews

A similar process is helpful whenever a new perspective is required – from seeing the world through Third World eyes, to understanding the point of view of First Nations residential school survivors. Here are some things to consider, then, when introducing a congregation to a vision that is broader and perhaps more complex than one they have had before.

- *Fill the pulpit with visitors.* Don't tell, show; that's every writer's rule. Most people dislike being lectured and they are smart enough, in any case, to figure out the point for themselves. The hooks that replaced the hands of activist Michael Lapsley, for example, displayed the power and evil of apartheid far more than any dozen sermons could. When he visited our congregation from South Africa, after a parcel bomb had almost killed him, his quiet faith led many in the congregation to see the world (and perhaps those who are disabled) in a new way. They listened carefully to his explanation of events in his troubled country, and to his prayers, and opened their hearts.

  And when lay minister Gerri Preston concluded the service by praying for compassion from the "God who has no other hands but ours," the congregation's collective recognition of Divine presence could have been defined in terms of the Emmaus Road.

- *Tackle tough issues with dignity and patience.* That's what happened at Sydenham Street United. The three co-chairs of the Affirming Congregation Study Group were highly respected: a lawyer and long-time member of the congregation, the father of a gay man who had died of AIDS, and the chair of the worship committee. Every month, one of them attended council to make a report and receive advice. Deliberate efforts were made to "lower the temperature," by communicating carefully. People were visited.

The elders, not the Affirming Congregation Study Group, were in charge of the voting process. And even now, despite its success and the length of the process, from the autumn of 1997 to May 1999, Hutchinson says that if he was involved in this process again, he "wouldn't go so fast."

- *But move when the moment is right.* Immediately after the September 11, 2001, destruction of the World Trade Center in New York City, Rev. Cheri di Novo at Emmanuel Howard Park United, in Toronto, immediately invited the members of the nearby mosque to their congregation. It was the beginning of a tender, flourishing relationship between the two groups.

- *Keep the image of movement present.* Long ago, when the Celtic monks embarked on a pilgrimage, it was not so much an effort to preach and convert (although those actions were often present) as it was to place themselves in the way of God.

  In one way, that's the purpose of a congregation. Author and Celtic expert Ian Bradley says that a "Christian emphasis on pilgrimage gives us today…a return to the ancient notion of Christians as people of (and on) the way." While this does not have to be a Celtic way, he says, "it does involve a self-understanding of Christians as travellers and voyagers, and a view of the church as essentially a provisional community."[9]

  It's hard to carry all your heavy "ideas, concepts, opinions and convictions" as Nouwen called them, when you leave your worldview behind and set out to an unknown destination.

- *Talk to each other in after-church forums.* Even with all this support, there will still be times when we won't feel like having our worldview expanded. Many people, like me, will want to turn off the news (part of the time, at least), tend to their nasturtiums, and avoid both the world's pain and its excitement. Preachers who focus solely, week after week, on themes of the world's anguish in worship will learn this to their sorrow.

But the news will not go away. A world climate change document published by the World Council of Churches, for example says that

In fact, life conditions are deteriorating… Change is not likely to come through persuasion. It may come as the dysfunctioning of the system becomes more and more obvious. *It will be accompanied by upheavals and suffering* [italics mine]. As we seek to re-define the meaning of sustainable development, this hard reality needs to be taken into account.[10]

Rather than overload Sunday worship, then, we need to make use of small groups, the great strength of congregations. And when we broaden our awareness in discussion, with an expert at hand to question, we also have each other – our community – to help us through our fear of "upheavals and suffering." Christian hope is what a congregation is about.

A Bible study group that refers to these issues is a good idea, too. We can face difficult news more cheerfully when we are sustained by the Good News. And the example and prayers and love of others around us gives us additional strength. We can marshal our words and be ready for the over-the-fence-conversations with the neighbors, as well as the letters, the protests, and the prayers that might change the world.

Because when we are with others, and our imaginations work together – and our hope is unleashed – we can have confidence. Like the disciples on the Emmaus Road inviting the stranger into their supper hour, we can suddenly recognize among us the living God, for whom nothing at all is impossible.

7

# The Life-Giving Congregation
## Leading for Others

So they came near the village to which they were going,
he walked ahead as if he were going on. But they urged
him strongly, saying, "Stay with us, because it is almost
evening and the day is now nearly over."
So he went in to stay with them.
Luke 24:28–29

**Christopher White**

**Vitality:** the ability to sustain life, vigor, liveliness, animation.
**Maturity:** with fully developed powers of body and mind, adult,
sensible, wise; completed natural development or growth.

On the surface, he would appear to be the last person you would choose as the ideal youth leader. In the midst of midlife, bearded and bald, United Church minister Ken Gallinger seems the polar opposite of the young, enthusiastic leader most churches think they need to build their youth ministry. But Ken has created one of this country's most vibrant youth programs. Actually, that's not completely accurate. What he has done is create within his congregation a multigenerational culture, where people of every age are encouraged and welcomed to share leadership. This has transformed his church and opened new venues of ministry for the whole congregation.

## New wine for new wineskins

For decades now, the church has embraced the weekly youth group model as *the* primary method of reaching out to youth and young adults. But it, like so many other institutions of the church, is predicated on a set of assumptions that are no longer valid in our world.

The first is that youth have lots of spare time on their hands for a weekly youth group meeting. This is simply no longer the case. Youth today are extraordinarily busy. Part-time jobs, sports, school, and arts activities take a tremendous amount of time.

Our own home is an example of this. I am writing this on what I call "Toxic Tuesday." I get Elizabeth to the arena at 4:00 p.m. for her skating lesson, watch her for 15 minutes, tear home, feed my eldest daughter, Sarah, drive her to the ballet studio, go back to the rink to get Elizabeth, drop her home, grab a quick bite, then leave again for a meeting. This kind of schedule is typical of most families in my congregation. When you add to that the ever increasing homework load, combined with the ever higher marks needed to get into post-secondary institutions, and the high cost of tuition which kids have to work to pay, it's wonderful that they find any time for church at all.

Youth are primarily peer driven. The influence of their classmates and the expectations of their friends have tremendous impact upon how they interact with the world. But their interaction with adults is, by and large, limited to parents and teachers – except at church. At church all generations intermix and it is in this intermixing that the future of youth ministry lies.

## Taking youth seriously

When Ken Gallinger arrived at First United in Mississauga almost ten years ago, he wanted, based on his experience elsewhere, to do something very different with the youth of this church. The key, in Gallinger's view, was to take the spiritual needs of teenagers seriously.

Everything else flows from that.

Taking the needs of people seriously was certainly central to Jesus' ministry. People who were deemed of low value in his society were the very people he spent the most time with. The Samaritan woman at the well, the lepers, the children, the poor – all of those on the "outside" Jesus welcomed. In the Emmaus Road story, Jesus certainly took the spiritual needs of the disciples seriously. The way that he did this is instructive. He did not reveal himself with a flash and a bang like a wizard in the latest Harry Potter movie. Instead, he asked the disciples questions – questions of compassion.

It is also important to watch how Jesus ministered to these people in their grief. He simply stayed with them, walked with them on their road, shared their home at night, and sat at table with them. Jesus provided a ministry of *presence*, taking them seriously and attending to their spiritual and emotional needs.

## Family-based youth ministries

Presbyterian minister Mark Devries is the author of *Family-Based Youth Ministry*. Based on his experience as a youth leader, Devries came to the conclusion that the traditional youth group model was broken. It was meeting the needs of the adults in the churches, but not of the young people themselves. So Devries wanted to find a different paradigm. The paradigm or model he settled on was the family – not the nuclear family, but the church as the family of God.

This "my family first" attitude, especially among Christians, has, in fact, only served to sever nuclear families from the very structures that can give their children lasting values and clear identity. Without strong ties to specific extended families, nuclear families have become self-perpetuating breeding grounds for rootlessness and alienation.[1]

Devries asserts that our youth are being neglected by adults, that we do not spend time guiding them to adulthood. Instead, we throw them to the wolves of adolescent culture with the result that

the lines between childhood and adulthood have become increasingly blurred, so much so that many adults well into their twenties still behave in a way characteristic of adolescents. With few clear rites of passage, teenagers are in the double bind of being expected to make adult decisions in a world that persistently juvenilizes them.[2]

For Devries, the solution is to create a youth ministry that does not segregate youth, but integrates them into the full life of the church. This means creating opportunities for youth and adults to interact.

## Liturgically hip?

The worship service can play a key role in this integration. Devries acknowledges that our worship may not completely meet the tastes of youth. "But sitting in worship is much like having a place to sit at the family dinner table. Whether the food is what you would have ordered or not, you eventually grow to like it, *and you know you belong* [italics mine]."[3]

It is this sense of belonging that is so central and so important for our youth. Yet I also believe that there are ways to make worship a positive experience for youth, without turning it into an MTV clone.

When I was on my sabbatical, I attended a congregation that has completely transformed their worship into a contemporary format: rock band, drama, the whole Willow Creek experience.

What struck me were the teenagers. I expected to see them up and clapping, moving to the music. But that was not what I saw. What I saw were youth with the same bored, angst-ridden expressions that can be found in any church in the land.

It is not the *form* of the worship, it is the *function* that youth play *in* the worship that engages them.

This has certainly proven to be the case at First United. The church's classic response, in Gallinger's view, has been to view adolescents as immature and unimportant, to not take seriously what teenagers are going through. Thus, the first goal for Gallinger was to create a community where teenagers' concerns would not be taken lightly. The question was what vehicle could he use to help the youth experience genuine community. His *and their* answer was music. He began a group called "The Liturgically Hip," a music group that embraced an eclectic and rich variety of music. It has proven to be a great success, with 53 young people involved and a waiting list to get in. This group participates regularly in worship, along with the senior choir and the children's choir. The group creates three to four major productions per year and has toured parts of Canada and the United States, and has even been to Cuba.

But important as that is, there is much more. The true impact of these teenagers can be seen in the church's structures. Youth do not simply sit as members of a youth committee; they participate fully in the board structure of their church. The congregation has placed youth in highly visible leadership roles, and then nurtured them for success. The chair of the spiritual development committee is 16 years old; the chair of the committee hiring their new musician is 18. Youth are hired as wedding hosts, responsible for setting up the church, running the wedding rehearsals, and taking responsibility for the couple. The approach has worked extremely well for everybody.

None of this has been done without effort. Gallinger not only integrates youth into worship, he makes sure that his preaching addresses the issues they are facing in their own lives. He works hard at keeping in contact with these kids. He's on MSN every afternoon checking in with them. He listens to their music and goes to see their films.

Without question, youth are high maintenance and it requires energy to deal with challenging and at times painful issues. But the results are worth it. In Gallinger's words, "These youth have enlivened the congregation, brought energy and joy to our church, and had a huge impact."

But where to start? What can you offer in a church that has only three to six teenagers?

For Gallinger, it comes down to respect. Respect those persons; "take seriously the few you have; understand that they are spiritual beings with spiritual needs." If you can do this, then you may find that you have more than only six youth members.

## "Aunt Helen"

There is another approach that churches with small numbers of teens can take. It is best exemplified by Willowgrove United, in Sault St. Marie, Ontario. Located in the Algoma Presbytery of the London Conference, Willowgrove has worked with their presbytery to create a youth ministry that encompasses that area's scattered rural churches. Under the direction of staff associate Helen Smith, a.k.a. "Aunt Helen," Algoma Presbytery has created a youth council that integrates youth into leadership at a presbytery and conference level.

"Belonging," says Smith, "is so important to these young people. They have a profound faith and deep dense of spirituality and they need to be really heard and respected."

The youth gather from across the presbytery regularly throughout the year. They mentor each other; create meaningful, authentic worship that they share with churches throughout the presbytery; and strike a balance between both service and fun.

In Smith's view, youth want to be treated no differently than any other group in the church. The church belongs to them as much as to anyone else, and they have lots to offer. Like Gallinger and Devries, Smith asserts that the old model of youth ministry will not work anymore. She believes that the pressures of school and the cost of post-secondary education have put a tremendous load on these young people. They need opportunities to blow off some steam and the presence of an adult who will truly take their needs seriously.

"Aunt Helen" has grown children of her own and brings the gifts of her experience to these young people. Her experience as a parent helps her in her work. Nothing the youth say or do has fazed her and they know that they can turn to her for advice, counsel, and support. She can also serve as an important bridge between the generations, both corporately in the church and within individual families.

## Diversity and involvement

While the forms may be new and the challenges different, the church has always struggled with "the youth question." Look at churches built in the 1920s in Toronto that had bowling alleys in their basements, or that set up pool tables to attract youth. Some issues are timeless.

The United Church has had for many years an organization called Canadian Girls in Training, or CGIT. While some people might snicker at it today, it is based on an important premise that sets it apart from any other secular organization for youth, including the Scouting movement. Their founding principle is articulated this way: "To be the girl that God would have me be."

Is that not what our goal in all ministry should be? To be the people that God would have us be? To help our young people develop into the adults that God would have them become? As stewards of our children, do we not have both the privilege and the responsibility to invest our best in the coming generation?

When I was growing up, I was part of the St. George's youth choir. This church group put on a Gilbert and Sullivan show each year and it was a wonderful experience for everyone involved. It created community, a sense of accomplishment, and was just plain fun. Not to mention the cast parties! It was through this group that I met my future spouse. For some people, music and drama is the vehicle that creates community. But not for all. For others, it may be sports, or computers, or church camps. We need to find ways of tapping into the diversity of interests our youth possess.

Perhaps the time has come for church leagues to make a comeback. Hockey, volleyball, and basketball all have a great draw. What an opportunity to use sports as a way of building ties with other faith communities, both Christian and those of other religions. The key, I believe, is twofold – a diversity of approaches and involvement in worship.

Since I interviewed Ken Gallinger, I have been attempting to put some of his and Mark Devries' ideas into practice. Our minister of music has begun a youth performance group that participates regularly in worship. We've begun an all-generations worship band that plays once a month, and youth are now regularly scheduled into the worship service as full participants.

We draw on some of our own traditions in this area and have experienced firsthand the impact that youth can have on us, and we on them. For ten years now, we have put on a Christmas Eve play, performed by our youth, at our 5:00 and 7:00 p.m. services. It has grown into quite a tradition, with close to 30 youth and adults involved in the production. Our younger kids grow up looking forward to the time when they can participate (Grade 7).

This past Christmas was our tenth anniversary and our last in our current facility, so I began a new tradition. As we sang our closing carol, *Silent Night*, we invited our alumni cast members to join us. What a parade it was of fine young adults, men and woman, all of whom benefited and were given lifelong positive memories of our church. That's what we need to try to give *all* young people – involvement, fun, and a sense that their needs are being seriously attended to. In the past two years, we have also hired our first youth coordinator, Marissa, a wonderful young adult who has grown our program tremendously while attending university and teacher's college. Currently, she has over 120 kids involved in our monthly senior and junior youth groups.

We are still a work in progress, but we are moving forward.

## Mr. Miagi?

When I interviewed Mark Devries and asked him what had changed since he first wrote his book in 1994, he told me that the church still has a great deal of anxiety and fixation around youth work. Like so many others in the church, those who are concerned about youth are also in search of the "magic potion" that will fill the church with happy enthusiastic young people. Alas, this magic potion or method simply doesn't exist.

Devries points out that one of the many challenges we now face is the question of what's normal? Parents *and* kids want to know what are normal expectations in behavior, clothes, and school. Any parent who has attempted to buy a pair of jeans for his or her daughter that do not come below her hips will appreciate this. So too will the parents of the son whose pants *have* to droop to the knees. And if the baseball cap ever comes off, watch out!

The influence of consumer culture on our young people is huge, says Devries, and the church "is like a cricket trying to stop a freight train." The answer, according to Devries, requires nothing less than creating our own culture within the churches. It is up to churches "to establish norms, to create a culture and a context, a new ethos to empower youth. It is like a series of locks for a ship; the water doesn't force the ship through; it allows the ship to rise. Too much of youth ministry seems to be about forcing the kids into programs and preset expectations."

Instead, we need to look at it from the needs and perspective of the young people we serve. The church, says Devries, is the one place where youth are surrounded by adults who don't care if they are the star of the hockey or soccer team, if they get straight A's, or if they are the most popular kids. We offer one thing that no one else can be, he asserts – Mr. Miagi.

Mr. Miagi is one of the characters in the 1980s movie called *The Karate Kid*. In the film, Mr. Miagi shows a young man, through repeated acts that seem unconnected and even trivial (such as painting the fence, painting the house, and waxing the car) how to use karate. In the process, the young man gains confidence, self-possession, and a feeling of his place in the world.

Jim Clendinning, a youth and family counselor, tells me that for an adolescent to make it happily and successfully to adulthood she or he needs one adult who cares deeply about them and invests time with them. For Devries, the church can be the place where this happens.

Devries' words are echoed in two other important publications: *The Godbearing Life: The Art of Soul Tending for Youth Ministry* and *Passing On the Faith: A Radical New Model for Youth and Family Ministry*. Both of these books echo Devries' belief that the current model needs to be reworked.

The key point these authors make is that the primary place of religious experience lies in the family. Likewise, the child's development, happiness, and ability to deal with life's challenges comes out of their experience with their family of origin. Hence, one of the church's key roles is to strengthen family relationships in whatever form they take.

Equally important is the role the church plays in creating an alternative church culture for our kids. The authors recognize that children today experience far more than did the previous generation. By the time a child graduates to high school in my community, they may have seen everything from divisive divorces, drugs and alcohol abuse, spousal abuse, eating disorders among their peers, and tragically, even suicide.

How do we provide support when we as families seem to spend far less time together?

One of our roles, as I mentioned earlier, is mentoring. In *The Godbearing Life*, authors Kenda Dean and Ron Foster say that

Of particular importance to adolescents is friendship with an adult who sees in them potential they do not necessarily see in themselves. Studies consistently indicate that a relationship with such an adult guarantor during adolescence outweighs all other forms of youth ministry in terms of positive influence on youth development.[4]

Like Jesus on the road to Emmaus, we as churches need to slow the frantic pace of our lives and simply *be* with our kids and each other. Whether it's in the church, the coffee shop, the mall, or the arena, wherever they need us to be is where we should minister. Another place to start is at table. As Helen Smith pointed out to me, how can kids who never eat as family understand the concept of the table and the full meaning of the Eucharist? In our own home, we have reinstituted Sunday night dinner. Candles on the table; the phone, television, radio, and computers turned off; we spend time eating, talking, and laughing together. It helps us reflect on the week that has gone by and prepare for the week ahead. We have also drastically curtailed eating in front of the television. By doing this, even in the midst of extremely busy schedules, we manage about four shared dinners per week. It has truly improved the quality of our lives.

Churches are evolving. The model that works for youth ministry is the model that works for your church. Start in one simple place, ask the kids what their needs are, and develop a ministry not out of what will work for you, but what will work for *them*.

## Heaven touches earth in worship

It was a hot, sultry Sunday evening in late June in downtown Toronto. I was in the company of three young adults from our church. We were on our way to attend an emerging generations church called Freedomize. I had learned about them through the United Church conference called Breakthrough, which had happened two weeks earlier. Held in the sanctuary of St. Andrew's Presbyterian, the experience more than caught my attention. I was probably the second oldest person in that service, which was packed with people in their 20s. The service was different than what I had expected. It was in the style of the Ancient Future movement. Candles, light and dark, communion, a band that played both new music and contemporary arrangements of traditional hymns. A long sermon, a long service. This was not an event programmed for the time conscious consumer.

This was countercultural worship. The theology and approach was postevangelical, very classically orthodox. Afterwards, when we went out to a café to debrief, I was anxious to hear the impressions of my three congregants. They loved the form, but the theology did not resonate with them. They were interested in seeing how we could do something that would more accurately reflect our context and meet the needs of their generation.

If the mainline church has struggled with what to do with youth, it has been almost silent about people in their 20s. While churches may have a youth minister, how many have one dedicated to young adults? Our unintentional pattern has been to say after graduation, "See you when you have kids and you want them baptized." We do little, if anything, to address the specific needs of this age group.

So a week after I attended worship at Freedomize, I went back into Toronto and had coffee with its 28-year-old senior pastor, Todd Cantelon. The interview itself was an experience of countercultural church. Let me share a couple of things Todd said that caught my attention:

- "Cultural relevance is irrelevant. We are not countercultural, we are anti-cultural."
- "We are not postmoderns, we are premoderns."
- "Classic youth ministry is babysitting."
- "The dance clubs are full of people in their 20s; the churches are empty."
- "Seeker-sensitive worship is garbage. People don't need pop."
- "Church doesn't come cheap. Expect sweat. Make it hard."

"Intense" would be one way of describing our time together, but certainly it was a refreshing approach.

Todd comes from a combination of Anglican and charismatic backgrounds and has spent his ministry working with youth and young adults. In our time together he quoted everything and everybody, including T. S. Eliot, the Nicene Creed, C. S. Lewis, and Dietrich Bonhoeffer. From Todd's perspective, there are two ways of approaching church for youth and young adults.

The first is what he calls "a church within a church" for youth. This means creating a parallel church for youth within an existing church. He tried this in 1994 and started with six kids. Within five months it had grown to almost 60 in worship, when it started to attract adults as well, causing a rift in the existing congregation. Todd saw this pattern happening in other places as well, so he decided to start a new church based solely on the needs of young adults. Freedomize is intensely membership driven; but instead of making it easy to join, Todd makes it very challenging – with a 13-week membership course, and the expectation of tithing and involvement. His approach goes against everything that churches have been told in the last decade about how to grow and attract new members. But it's working: 80% of his growing congregation of 20-somethings are brand new to the Christian church. Cantelon's church challenges them; it both expects and gives a lot. The result is steady slow growth.

Why is it working? I believe we are all born to worship. We all worship. But we choose what we worship. Equally, we choose the story upon which we base our lives, the story which gives our lives color and context, the story that fills our bones with meaning. Cantelon makes the Christian story real to this emerging generation.

People are looking for something to base their lives upon and the secular story of consumerism is not enough. People don't simply want comfort, they want edge. We in the mainline need to rediscover the Christian edge, those parts that grate against the culture, that define our distinctiveness.

That, I believe, is the approach for people in their 20s. Challenge them, embrace them with opportunity, not to serve on a committee, but to have a life changing experience. If our churches don't offer them that then why would they come? As with youth, the challenge is to integrate them into our multigenerational life by taking their needs seriously.

Walk with your youth and young adults as Jesus walked with those disciples on the Emmaus Road, and together, as the family of God we may transform our lives and just maybe our world.

# The Obedient Congregation
## Walking with the Artist

Were not our hearts burning within us while he was
talking to us on the road, while he was opening
the scriptures to us?
Luke 24:32

**Donna Sinclair**

**Obedience:** 1. The practice or condition of being obedient,
the act of obeying.
2. Pertaining to ecclesiastical authority or a group
of people under such authority.

Sometimes the one who walks beside us on the Emmaus Road is the artist – the poet, painter, musician, singer. If the church existed for no other reason than to offer a place for the arts to flourish, that would be enough. Because we are all, every single one of us, artists when we are in church. Art restores memory, creates cosmos out of chaos (like God does) and lets us express the inexpressible, that for which there is no words. Art lets us imagine possibility, so that we can make a better world. Art lets us talk to God.

We need to acknowledge how crucial it is to have the arts flourish in our congregations and we need to allow it to happen.

Note that the operative word is "allow." We are by nature a story-telling, music-singing, picture-making, fabric-weaving-quilting species. All we have to do is say yes.

Consider first, going to Sunday worship.

We walk down the aisle. Immediately, we are in contemplation of the story. In many, especially older, buildings, it appears in colored glass, a reminder of the days when few could read and the important narratives of faith were outlined in the windows. In other buildings, it may be found in quilts or banners or even mobiles or sculpture. There may be depictions of Jesus, Bibles and roses, lilies and crowns of thorns, doves and flames, Greek letters and crosses. We have entered a gallery of symbolism, are assaulted on all sides by the marvelous narrative we hold in common, the one that keeps us together and gives us strength, day after day, to face the world.

Even if this were all, perhaps it would be enough to sustain our faith.

But there is more. The service begins. There is music. There is a prayer, a collection of words chosen for the ears of God, the best words we can find, little chunks of poetry. Immediately the world's chaos begins to fall away and our souls begin to emerge like groundhogs after a long winter. By the time we stand for the first hymn, we have become part of a stylized and ancient drama, the liturgy that connects us with past and present. The choir has come in, robed (or in contemporary services, perhaps informally dressed) and so has the minister; a candle has been lit, perhaps. This is God's own theatre, our performance for God's eyes.

And then we sing. For many of us, this will be the only time all week that we sing. Even warbling in the shower has begun to seem more-or-less unnecessary; we have radios in the bathroom. But here, we sing words of beauty, to tunes of beauty, and chaos is pushed a little further back.

Most of us do our best at this, even if the world does not call us gifted. The words seep into us, our cells made permeable to them by the music. Sometimes, a junior choir will sing, their small voices reaching hearts that have grown already, this early in the liturgy, more vulnerable and more open to the Spirit.

There will be a sermon, usually with a prayer to begin. "The Lord be in my lips and in my speaking." Here is prayer as possibility. Couldn't all our spoken words be like that, with God in them?

We will listen to the choir. In my congregation, some members – even the most uncharismatic – shut their eyes and sway a little, letting the music carry them. It is a moment of power, when the mingled voices become more than the sum of all of them, when the sound that emerges is often sweet, and ringing like angels. Perhaps not always, but in every congregation there is at least once a moment of purity and clarity and light.

(On a visit to New York City, I attended Sunday morning worship in an historic Presbyterian church, a tiny old building jammed between skyscrapers, incongruous and faded and beautiful. The choir consisted of two, frail, elderly sopranos, and their voices wavered. But their faces were full of light. Their age had made them very close to God.)

As the service proceeds, more prayers will be offered, usually from a layperson, sometimes one skilled with words, sometimes not. No matter. This prayer, in its reaching for the words to address God, becomes a poem. More hymns are sung, and we rise and sit, rise and sit, by now fully part of the story we have come to enter – the story of the God who fell to earth and rose again, bringing us with him. While we are here, in this building, we believe this. The world outside is without knowledge of this truth.

As the two disciples said, "Wasn't it like a fire burning within us...?"

Of course it is. As theologian John Dominic Crossan says, we are always on the road to Emmaus. There is nowhere else we go each week, except church, where we sing and say poems, and sit in the light of visual arts, in glass and paint, and feel "the fire burning within us." We are like those two disciples, "when he talked to us on the road and explained the scriptures to us..."

We don't always know this, when we are there. But it's true.

## What is this art for?

According to much-loved author Madeleine L'Engle, it helps us remember. "In art we are once again able to do all the things we have forgotten; we are able to walk on water; we speak to the angels who call us; we move, unfettered, among the stars."[1]

Art helps us remember that we are creators, a role adults have so harshly been taught to forget. Christians "are to be in this world as healers, as listeners and as servants," says L'Engle. We need those skills in a world that threatens to overwhelm us with implacable terrors – global warming inching toward us, the endless fear so many people play on that our borders will breached, that we will be overrun with people-not-like-us, that there will be white powder in the mail.

But here, the world can't touch us. We sing, dreaming, of the winds of God, of a blood-red flag carrying us to freedom and hope. This is the furthest thing from escapism. It is the sustaining of a belief that a world in pain can be different; that we can help create it differently.

The arts of worship embed the hope of our great story in us. As Dawn Vaneyk, a minister in Sudbury, Ontario, tells it, it may not always go smoothly. But it doesn't matter.

It was the day before Valentine's Day – Samson and Delilah were the topic. I got to church and the music director told me that the organist had called in sick. Mary Kay Morris would pinch-hit. Not sure if we would have either anthem. She'd let me know. It was Communion Sunday. A few new council members had never served here before and were a bit nervous.

Just before the service, I realized that two Eucharistic prayer files had got mixed together. Some people had the right one for the day – others did not.

So at the beginning of the service I named each of these dilemmas and said that it had been suggested (by the music director), that we start the service with a disclaimer. (They all chuckled, warmly.) So I said that what the Holy Spirit willed, we would ride with. (Smiles.)

We got through the first part of the service. All went well until the reader left out an entire chapter that was the center of the Samson story.

No problem. I read it before the sermon.

We sang the Eucharistic hymn and the usher went down to get the kids up for communion. We waited. They straggled in. We waited for the junior choir. They didn't appear. I slipped down to the organist and asked for a hymn: *What a Friend We Have in Jesus.* They still didn't appear. Slowly they, too, straggle in. (Seems one Sunday school teacher had trouble wrapping up, and then they took forever getting their gowns on [gotta look good!!], and then one young girl just couldn't get into her right place in line.)

We take a moment and make sure everyone has access to the right Eucharistic prayer. We thank God. I declare: "Come! For all things are ready!" The servers get up and move over to the table. A voice whispers in my ear, "You forgot the junior choir anthem." Out of the corner of my eye, I see the music director already up (having caught her gown on the corner of the choir loft), so I verily shout, "Sit! For all things are NOT ready!" The servers retreat.

The children sing. Finally, a sense of holiness descends upon the proceedings. We eat and drink. Some are anointed with prayers for healing. We are commissioned. We sing *Sing a Happy Hallelujah!* On the way out, the pinch-hitting organist (who never missed a beat) declared that it was, indeed, the thirteenth!

Sheepishly, I greeted people at the door. Outrageously, several declared what a wonderful service it had been! Later, I heard that *What a Friend* was someone's mother's favorite hymn and that they had been thinking of her that morning. Two teenagers apparently spent lunch discussing the various aspects of the Samson story. The Holy Spirit lives, sister, that's all I can say![2]

Vaneyk knows that all is acceptable to God and that the artists' integrity and quality of spirit, not technique, are what count.

## A dozen things to know about the arts in church

• It is fine to spend money on art for church (though not to the exclusion of financing social justice). The lovely painting that covers the back wall of our sanctuary depicts large and small people being blessed by Jesus. These crowds of children and adults, Native and non-Native, women and men, in modern dress, always remind me of who I am and why I am here. I am blessed, grateful, along with all these others. Prayer is sometimes formed in paint, as well as in words.

- The arts, as they express our faith, are infinitely various. It is crucial not be caught in one understanding of what God loves, or in one notion of what feeds our spiritual hunger. Of course church art can be glorious – Bach, Handel, Mozart. But as Winnipeg artist, poet, and minister Bob Haverluck points out in his three-act radio play *Glory to God in the Lowest*, God loves just as much the art of the humblest among us, the ones who cannot afford pipe organs and choir gowns.

  What if, says Haverluck, "the little Chilean cloth murals of resistance and celebration (*arpilleras*); or the people's theatre of the oppressed; or the singable songs of group protest; or the street murals and posters of artist gangs are paradigms of culture through which God's words tumble out and sing gracefully?"[3]

  That would give powerful meaning to the little group, their voices sometimes ragged with the cold, singing outside their local MP's office. Perhaps these peace vigils – with the candles that flicker and die in the wind, that are held by folk who may or may not find themselves at home in a congregation, but who yearn for the world to be whole – perhaps this is a new and liberating form of church. It is in the streets, Haverluck goes on, in the "church halls and back rooms of Winnipeg, Chicago, Santiago that artworks for emancipation smoulder…"

- Be wary, then, of censorship. That follows from the note above. Haverluck's argument also gives new meaning to the somewhat-controversial Christmas pageant staged one year in our congregation, about a single young mom named Mary, living on the street with Joe. It also gives new meaning to the many years the pageant was turned over to the youth, who became increasingly experimental. A wise congregation clings with one hand to loved tradition, and with the other to the understanding that God is not easily shocked.

- There is great delight in being present at the creation. That's why Hollywood movie clips in church – while fun and often moving – are not as holy as the piece of theatre in which young and old church members are together, dressed up in handmade costumes, creating drama from the heart. A drama that – no matter how often it is performed – is always unique to these people and this place, this little community of God. Christmas pageants, Easter pageants, and chancel dramas bind us to one another in faith.

- The Christian story must come to life inside of us. That's what faith is. Church drama is one of the very best ways to make that happen. The biblical characters become real in us when our son plays Joseph, our daughter plays Mary, the newest baby in the congregation plays the baby Jesus. This newness of life never goes away. The child is born to all of us, again and again. And after a while, we recognize him, breaking bread, sitting beside us. He is the street person who wanders in looking for the food bank, the neighbor with whom we quarreled last year, the spiritual elder passing us the grape juice.

- Storytellers are a great asset. Most cities have a group, who can be invited (as individuals or together) to offer their talent. Let those who understand in their bones what story is retell the gospel narratives. It will be as if you are hearing them for the first time. L'Engle says that a friend of hers told her, "Jesus was not a theologian. He was God who told stories."[4]

- Say thank you to the artists, as often as you can. It is good to be obedient to the art, each of us as individuals, when we can. But art asks a great deal of us, so it is not always possible to do that in a large way. It takes time to sew those costumes at the busiest time of year. It takes discipline to turn out to choir practice, week after week, when other things are pressing. We need to cherish those who do that for us.

(Which is a good time to note that the question of whether or not to clap in church after the anthems, or even during a well-written sermon, does not merit the controversy it evokes in some congregations. If it's a way of saying "thank you" to the artist, it's a good idea. If it's a judgment on the quality of the piece, to be withheld at various times, it's not a good idea. Congregations might discuss sometime what they mean by it, and go with that.)

- It is wise to cherish what we already have and not let it slip away. Sometimes – in a world so full of glossy performance in the movies or on TV – we think that the little things we do in church are nothing. But they are ours. They are wrapped around our own ancient and present story. They are *everything*.

- True art means taking risks. Dawn Vaneyk (in her conclusion that "The Holy Spirit lives, sister, that's all I can say!") knows that. In fact, most ministers risk, every Sunday, that the junior choir won't be quite robed, or the reader quite ready. That's part of what makes it art.

  We see this in Bob Haverluck's drawings too. Street people as angels; lovers threatened by King Solomon's soldiers; blue-stained berry pickers, rejoicing in God's unfenced, unowned bounty. The artist takes a risk in helping us see what we could not previously see. If we as audience miss the point, for example, we may grumble. But when we recognize what is before us (as Cleopas could attest), it lifts our hearts with joy.

- Above all, true art means doing our best, singing our best. It may be flawed. But all God wants is our best, not perfection. In return, we are given strength. In occupied East Germany, in 1987, I heard the lonely beauty of a single clarinet in church. In a country with a powerfully atheistic government, where church meetings were often attended by a member of the secret police, they found a way to make the arts sustain their faith – a faith that gave churches the courage to help topple the Berlin Wall two years later.

- Cherish and sustain church artists. Our congregation (like others, although we like to feel we are unique) is richly blessed by our choir director. Ralph Johnston writes marvelous music and inspired lyrics. (That sounds like overstatement, but there are no other words.) Sometimes he gathers the yearnings of the people of our region, placing the coming of Christ in the winter snow. Sometimes he gathers images so universal they could be sung in the Sahara.

    If the job of this congregation, and others, was only to support this kind of expression, it would be enough. But of course, there is more. And in return, Johnston's vision (and that of musicians in so many congregations) sustains the faith of those who carry out the gospel's commandments in other ways.

- Honor the art of children. As L'Engle says, they know something about creativity and imagination that adult Christians must remember, if they are to serve the world with hope. Hang it in the sanctuary, or the entrance. Frame or back it properly, as we would an adult's art. Display the names and titles. The artist should be properly identified. Take the art down before it is frayed. Return it if you can, or warn in advance if you cannot. As always, thank the artist, with a proper letter, on church letterhead.

## Conclusion

None of this is new. Most congregations will recognize themselves in this discussion. But perhaps we don't consider often enough how precious congregations are, as carriers of the arts in the very best sense. We are patron and artist and actor all at once. And – with God – we are the audience. It is like a fire burning within us, helping us remember who we are.

# 9

# The Curious Congregation
## Learning from Others

Then he said to them, "Oh, how foolish you are, and
how slow of heart to believe all that the prophets have
declared! Was it not necessary that the Messiah should
suffer these things and then enter into his glory?" Then
beginning with Moses and all the prophets, he interpreted
to them the things about himself in all the scriptures.

Luke 24:25–27

### Christopher White

**Curiosity:**    an eagerness and desire to know.
**Conversation:**  the informal spoken exchange of ideas.

From the moment of the very first Easter, the embryonic Christian community engaged the Bible. They studied the Hebrew scriptures in an attempt to understand who Jesus was; they studied it to place themselves in its overarching story of hope. The Bible was for them a living entity through which they lived, breathed, and found themselves.

Throughout the gospels, Jesus engages scripture as a central part of his ministry. It's so central that it is even included in the Easter experience. It is only through this exchange that the disciples on the Emmaus Road are able to find meaning in Jesus' life, death, and resurrection.

So too, in our churches today, we recognize how important the Bible is to us. We read it aloud and preach from it each Sunday in worship. We spend enormous energy and effort making sure that the coming generation is grounded in its core stories. Extensive curricula are created, workshops held, teachers trained, and websites built, all dedicated to children and youth. So why, when we spend all that effort on our children, do we not spend equal amounts on our adult population?

Granted, there have been numerous Bible studies published and congregations have spent hours immersing themselves in them. Traditionally, the two that seem most familiar to mainline congregations have been the Bethel and Kerygma series.

Bethel is perhaps the oldest and has been used by over a million people in its 40-year history.

Rooted in the conservative Lutheran tradition, Bethel is intensely teacher driven and requires the minister and/or lay trainer to attend a week-long education session on the course. They, in turn, train a teaching team that is committed to spending two and a half hours per week with the material. Two years later, they are then ready to offer six, seven-week sessions to the congregation. The focus of Bethel is the whole Bible. The format is fairly formal, with tests and quizzes to keep participants up to speed. The program is lay-driven and brings a conservative perspective to scripture. Bethel maintains that while it teaches the Bible, parish clergy provide the theological content from their local perspective.

On the other end of the continuum sits the Kerygma Bible study. Used by over 30 denominations since its inception in 1977, Kerygma offers a variety of approaches. There is a 34-part study of the whole Bible, or you can partake of one of the many seven-week sessions on books of the Bible, or on a particular theme; for example, the Psalms, or a study of the scripture in Handel's *Messiah* or Brahms' *Requiem*. Kerygma is based on the following core theological principles.

> Scripture should be allowed to speak for itself. If the Bible is understood on its terms, it will convey its own truth. Biblical understanding should be a prelude to theological belief. The Bible should inform theology, not theology the bible."[1]

These two Bible studies are in as wide use today as they once were. In their place, church school curricula such as *Seasons of the Spirit* (and *The Whole People of God* before it) and *Bible Quest*, have integrated adult study materials into their programs. This has the advantage of making learning a "whole family" based activity. It also serves to link the worship life and learning life together.

But there is another option making its presence felt and it dwarfs all other adult Christian education programs.

## Alpha, Alpha, everywhere

Alpha has been the most successful adult Christian education program in the history of the church. It has traveled to 132 countries, been translated into 36 languages, and, as I write, is taking place in 24,178 venues around the globe. It has crossed the divisions between evangelical, Catholic, and mainline congregations, and has revitalized churches all over the world.

Like the ubiquitous "Chicken Soup for every soul on earth" book series, this program has adapted and remodeled itself to meet some of the most diverse needs in the world. There is Alpha for prisons, the armed forces, students, and youth.

If Christianity has a brand name, it's Alpha. Its trademark question mark, held by a struggling little man, and its uniformity of content and delivery, make it instantly recognizable. In a culture where people have been trained to flock to brand outlets and chains like The Gap, there is tremendous comfort in the known and the familiar. For clergy and churches seeking programs, not only for their own congregation, but to reach out to the wider community, Alpha seems irresistible.

The program is a complete package. A video of the very accessible, friendly, articulate, and genuinely amusing Nicky Gumbel is shown each session. Gumbel gently communicates his own doubts and struggles, and shows that church is not everything you were afraid it was going to become. Manuals that break down every task that needs to be performed are provided, as are outlines of questions for group leaders to ask, and even recipes for the dinners.

In addition, books are available, such as Gumbel's *Telling Others* and *Questions of Life* that tackle the faith-based issues we all face. There are also 25-page booklets that cover every topic from Christmas to the question of suffering.

To be honest, Alpha is also fun – something that has been sorely lacking in our programs to date, which may have been earnest, but rarely truly enjoyable.

So everything is there for the church and the clergy. More importantly, Alpha is teacher-proof; no one, without enormous effort, can wreck it. It is the closest thing we may ever have to a bulletproof program. Who wouldn't want to run it in their churches? As one Anglican priest said, "If you want to grow your church, use Alpha."

Still, I have to say that our church chose to go in a different direction. When I first heard about Alpha, I was very excited and thought that this was just what our church needed to kick-start our adult Christian education program. For years we had struggled, putting on the typical Advent and Lenten series, plus the occasional Bible study, with less than stunning results. So I was eager and willing to embrace this program. I purchased a sampling of the resources, called our Christian education committee together for a meeting, and talked to colleagues who had used it. As we reviewed the material together, my initial enthusiasm began to cool and our committee expressed significant reservations. Why?

With Alpha, not only do you have to buy the marketing package, but for the program to work, you also have to buy the theological package, lock, stock, and barrel. That's the reason why we do not use it in our congregation.

Alpha arose out of the charismatic tradition of the Anglican Church. Gumbel himself has been strongly influenced by the Toronto Blessing group. Thus, his understanding of the Holy Spirit comes from that tradition. Speaking in tongues and the born-anew experience are very much a part of the Holy Spirit weekend that completes the course.

Personally and congregationally, those things do not resonate with our experience or theology. Nor are we comfortable portraying them as the primary model for how people experience the Spirit of God.

Even more troubling, though, from my own perspective is Gumbel's approach to other religions. In his publication *What about Other Religions?* he asks the question, "Is Jesus the only way to God?"

The answer of the New Testament is an emphatic "yes"...
The fact that Jesus is the only way to God does not mean that we simply write off all other religions as misguided or demonic...Indeed we would expect to find truth in other religions...By putting other religions alongside God's revelation in Jesus Christ, we see that they contain both truth and error. There is a dark side to other religions. There may be a dark side to the way that some people use Christianity, but there is no dark side to God's revelation in Jesus Christ.[2]

I do not find that theological perspective helpful as I try to discern how best to live with my neighbors in the 21st century. As I and others have written elsewhere, interfaith relations are *the* issue of the new millennium. Humility and compassion need to be the twin characteristics of the Christian faith.

Jesus is my way to God. Jesus is how I understand and see God. But to insist that he is the *only* way is to reap a whirlwind of misunderstanding and potential conflict. It also places God in a box not of our Creator's making.

So what do we do? At Westminster, we have created some alternatives that have worked for us, but before exploring them, I believe we need to take a more serious look at how adults learn.

## A flute and a doctorate

Pandora Bryce has a PhD in music education and travels around the globe, running workshops on education theory and practice. In addition, she is a professional flautist who has performed across North America. Pandora has lived her life with music. Her religious background is eclectic. As a teenager, she was involved in a charismatic church, then moved to a high Anglican congregation. After being away from all churches for many years, she is slowly integrating herself into a United Church. Her critique of the charismatic experience is that, "You must be willing to submit who you are to that [Charismatic] worldview. Everything is seen through that view and you must be willing to let go of your personal experience. If you do, it's a wonderful, safe haven."

That is exactly why I had difficulty with Alpha.

As an educator of adults, Bryce has written and taught about how and why adults learn. According to her, adult learners have specific characteristics.

- Adults filter new learning through the lens of their experience.
- Adults are more interested in whether new learning fits their self-concept.
- Adults learn best without time pressure.
- Adults need to learn quickly and apply it to their real life.

- Past experience is always a part of adult learning.
- Adults may react to new information by becoming defensive and resistant.
- Adults like to learn in ways that have already worked for them.
- Adults need clear directions, specific objectives, and feedback.[3]

Andragogy, the theory of teaching adults, is a fairly new discipline. As coauthors M. S. Knowles, E. F. Holton III, and R. A. Swanson show in their book *The Adult Learner*, its precepts are completely different than those of pedagogy, which deals with the teaching of children:

**Adults need to know why they need to learn something.**
The first task of the facilitator is to help the learners become aware of the "need to know."

**Adults maintain the concept of responsibility for their own decisions, their own lives.**
[A]dult educators…make efforts to create learning experiences in which adults are helped to make the transition from dependant to self-directed learners.

**Adults enter the educational activity with a greater volume and more varied experiences than do children**.
Hence, the emphasis in adult education is on experiential techniques…in any situation in which the participants' experiences are ignored or devalued, adults will perceive this as rejecting not only their experience, but rejecting themselves as persons.

**Adults are life-centered in their orientation to learning.**
Adults are motivated to learn to the extent that they perceive that learning will help them perform tasks or deal

with problems that they confront in their life situations. Furthermore, they learn new knowledge, understandings, skills, values, and attitudes most effectively when they are presented in the context of application to real-life situations.

**Adults are more receptive to internal motivators than external motivators**.

All normal adults are motivated to keep growing and developing, but this motivation is frequently blocked by barriers such as negative self-concept as a student, inaccessibility of opportunities and resources, time constraints…[4]

The authors go on to make the point that

Andragogy's core adult learning principles take the learner seriously. They go beyond basic respect for the learner and view the adult learner as a primary source of data for making sound decisions regarding the learning process.[5]

The challenge as we design adult Christian education programs is to keep these concepts as a central part of the experience.

## Dinner and a movie

One of Alpha's key components is how they prepare the group to learn and interact together. The heart of that process lies in the meal that is served before the program. As Christians, the table is central to our identity; we gather around it for community and we share our sacraments upon it.

Having a meal together breaks down barriers and relaxes everyone. It is a wonderful way of coming together.

When I ran, using United Church materials, an adult confirmation and education program, which I called "Christianity 101," we started with a prepared dinner. The results were wonderful. Greater numbers attended the program than in previous attempts and the participation of the people was outstanding. Instead of rushing in the door with our day's stress trailing behind us, we were able to relax, get to know one another, and when the program started we were receptive to its content.

Likewise, when I created a four-week program called "Omega" this past fall, dinner was an integral part of the evening. I also attempted to utilize as many of these key adult learning concepts as possible. The subjects we covered were "God and Jesus," "What Happens When I Die?" "Interfaith Dialogue," and "The Church, the Body of Christ."

I utilized a variety of resources from film clips, to Marcus Borg, to Philip Yancey. We had large- and small-group interaction, guided questions, and a case study. Omega was very successful and will, I hope, be the template for a larger project.

But it was missing something. In fact, every program I have ever been a part of had one, key component missing. That component was a practical application to be utilized during the program itself.

My coauthor, Donna Sinclair, pointed me in a direction to fill that gap. Over 20 years ago, her church ran a study under the direction of Rev. John Harries, entitled *An Experiment in Practical Christianity*. In many ways, it was a precursor to a mainline Alpha.

The program was biblically based, included a shared meal each week, and ended with a retreat. "An Experiment in Practical Christianity" changed the lives of those who participated in it.

What made it unique was that the participants utilized an "experiment" in Christianity during the course. Donna's group took a trip to a funeral home, toured the facility, and spoke to the funeral director about preparing for death.

The experiment took people deep into the texts of the Bible. Acting out the scriptures they were studying was an integral part of the program and Sinclair recalls how it affected her on one occasion.

> I was acting out the part of Jairus' daughter and being brought back to life as a 12-year-old girl. As she was being brought back, I realized that there was a part of *me* that needed to be brought back, the part of me that could have fun, that could giggle… It changed my life.

We need life changing experiences like that in adult Christian education, experiences that help us find out who we are, experiences that bring us closer to God and to one other. We need programs that integrate our faith into our actual lives, that give us an opportunity to not simply *learn* about our faith, but to *do* it.

A few years ago, I read a phrase that I cannot attribute, but that sums it all up for me. What we need to help people develop is a faith with "spiritual depth and intellectual integrity." It is what Jesus gave to those disciples on the Emmaus Road and it is what each of us needs in order to navigate our own roads.

# The Generative Congregation
## Walking with Our Elders

*...beginning with Moses and the writings of
all the prophets...*
Luke 24:27

**Donna Sinclair**

**Integrity:**    unwavering adherence to a strict moral or ethical code.
The quality or condition of being whole or undivided;
completeness.
**Generativity:** includes in its wider sense the mature drive to generate
and regenerate products and ideas... Wisdom is the
virtue of the last crisis.[1]

We were at Tatamagouche, a lovely Christian education
center near Truro, Nova Scotia, on September 11, 2001.
It was a gathering of the national women's group of our
denomination, with representatives from all over Canada. I was making
notes, getting ready to write a story on their work. Then the director of
the center, uncharacteristically grave-faced, suddenly appeared in the

meeting room. The World Trade Center in New York had been hit by planes piloted by suicide terrorists, he explained; lower Manhattan was in chaos; North American air space was shut down. Even as he spoke, passenger planes diverted from routes all over the continent were filling the runways at Halifax, Nova Scotia, and Moncton, New Brunswick.

Those planes would sit there for days, while our suddenly small, North American world tried to deal with the innocent dead, and a new (although familiar to much of the rest of the world) feeling. Vulnerability.

I worried about the older women among us. How would they cope? A few would remember the Korean War, or even, as children, the Second World War. And here they were, stranded far from home, not knowing when or how they would return.

My fears were groundless. The women assimilated the news, talked quietly about what it could mean, and expressed their concern for the families. Emily Robertson, from Montreal, gathered everyone in a circle and we prayed for a very long time.

And then the women went calmly back to their meeting. I continued to scribble notes. For the moment, they had done all that they could do; they had pleaded with God for compassion for the families of those hurt or killed, and they had got on with life.

Months later, at another event, again with a high proportion of older women, I asked for their advice to young women, in the light of this (to us) changed world. "Don't panic," they said, variously. "Pray." "Trust in God." "Do not be afraid."

It was the wisdom of elders. Like Jesus reaching back to Moses and the prophets as he talked with Cleopas and the other disciple, they, too, can reach back into the past for insight. The elders among us had survived a world war, the death of friends, entire nations under enormous stress.

## The gifts of our elders

Now, more than ever, we need our elders. This chapter is about what they have to teach us, and why we often find it hard to listen. It's also a plea against congregations segmenting themselves too strenuously into young and old: contemporary worship for the young and hip, traditional worship for the superannuated whose ways are almost gone.

While we dispense with the inconvenience of having to listen to each other's music and voices, we lose some crucial things: the virtue of our elders' care for the next generations, which famed psychologist Erik Erickson labeled "generativity." We also lose the wisdom of those who have almost lived out their lives. Wisdom, again in Erickson's terms, is "the detached and yet active concern with life itself in the face of death itself, [which] maintains and conveys the integrity of experience in spite of the disdain over human failings and the dread of ultimate non-being."[2]

The elder women at Tatamagouche, in their combination of compassion and calm in the face of disaster, epitomized – out of their long lives – that integrity of experience, that detached and yet active concern with life in the face of death.

## The gift of care

Our elders care for our children (and us) in a special way. They love us. When my children were little, many years ago, two "generative" and wise members of the congregation, Esther and Murray Mason, often volunteered to look after them. My husband, Jim, and I were a busy young couple. The Masons were retired, and had a farm, and blackberry bushes, and in the fall, lots of fresh-pressed apple juice in their big warm kitchen – a perfect environment for our two very active small boys.

One spring day they went fiddlehead picking – David and Andy, aged three and five; and Murray and Esther Mason. Picking these fresh, young, tightly curled ferns is an enterprise that's full of mud; fiddleheads like to grow on the shallow marshy turns of an old creek.

When the boys were returned to us, tired and happy and clutching great bags of the early greens, both were wide-eyed. They had crossed a great river, David explained, miles and miles of water.

"Mmm," I said. "I guess you must have got your feet wet."

"Oh, no," he said. "Murray had his big boots on, and he walked across the water and his arms were full of me."

Another time, we had dinner at their big farmhouse in the warm kitchen. It was winter and after the meal, as the moon rose, Murray and Esther urged Jim and me onto cross-country skis. While the children were read stories by their Mason surrogate grandparents, this too-busy young couple flew over moonlit trails, utterly intoxicated by snow and moon – and leisure, a concept we had forgotten. The next day we solidified this learning by purchasing skis.

All this, I think, taught us to be generative in our turn. Many years after our adventures with Esther and Murray, in another province, I received this letter from a young mother from our congregation who had moved away.

Our year continues to be an adventure and a wonderful time of growing. In three days we move into our new home, with our family all together and our home comforts, much missed over the last year.

I've just come back from a weekend filled with laughter and tears, stories and songs, dance and hope – a women's retreat weekend in the foothills of the Rocky Mountains. As I was being driven home, my mind dizzy with the weekend's experiences, my thoughts brought me back to my "cloud of witnesses."

Your family was central in my thoughts and I experienced a yearning to let you know how important a role you have played in my life – what wonderfully solid people you have been for a terribly needy young woman. You have modeled for me parenting, marriage, friendship, faith, and action. I was coming from a place of blindness and feel so grateful for my eyes being opened in the midst of such love and safety. You taught me by example. I want to share with you more of my journey, but for now I needed to let you know of my gratitude for guidance, both when you knew you were guiding – but especially when you didn't.[3]

I had no idea. But of course, I am an elder now, just as Esther and Murray had been for us. Becoming an elder in this sense is not an articulated or planned event. It just happens.

But it can't happen if we separate the congregations' generations so thoroughly they never get to sing together, or pray together or visit over coffee after church or drop by Sunday afternoon with perennials from the garden.

## Our elders carry the traditions

The collective memory of our people helps us discern the proper action to undertake in times of stress. The Wesleyan Quadrilateral (much-quoted, I note, in my own denomination at times of stress) has "tradition" as one of its four tools for discernment.

Tradition is important. I know this from my Jewish daughter-in-law, Joan, when she quietly insisted she learn to make the Christmas bread. It was the first holiday home after she and David were engaged, and she knew about tradition. So she and I worked in the kitchen, shaping the bread that had been the sign of celebration in our family for years, shaped in a circle like a wreath, stuffed with raisins and cinnamon.

I fell completely in love with her that day; with the honor she paid to a loving custom that was not her own, but which she was committed to keeping alive. In a way, that's also what a congregation does; it honors traditions that we may not fully understand, but will keep alive because we love the bearers of it.

(Traditions are, of course, meant to be bent. I suspect Joan will find a lower-calorie way of making that bread. And, given the Passover recipes she just sent me, I too have new traditions to learn.)

In our congregation, traditions shift. The pageant changes from year to year. The baptismal font is no longer filled before the service, but during it, by a horde of small people carrying symbolic jars of water. A new stained-glass window depicts northern pines, in memory of a much-loved forester. The candles for the candlelight service at Christmas are now housed in long holders suspended above the people, a nod to our need for more light and more safety.

But we are sustained by continuities. When we settle into our places, year after year, there are the same hopeful, flickering lights; the same timeless words of baptism, the water pouring, the child named, just as the child's father and grandmother and great-grandparents were named. Our elders remember how it is done. This gives us strength.

## Our elders have the long view

You don't get complete calm in the face of adversity until you are old. It's called wisdom. Again, turning to Erickson's definition, wisdom is a kind of detachment from the present, an ability to place it within a long narrative of similar crises from which we have recovered. Years ago, my husband served a primarily English-speaking congregation in Quebec. When a beloved staff associate was leaving – it happened to coincide with the election of a separatist provincial government, which made many Anglo-Quebeckers feel vulnerable and alone – numerous church members expressed sadness and fear. Murray Mason rose to his feet in a board meeting. He named other times when it seemed the congregation might die. And it hadn't. And it didn't; it's still strong 25 years later.

## Why we sometimes can't hear

But sometimes the elders of the congregation are hard to listen to. It's because they live, partly, in a different world. Author and scholar Carolyn Heilbrun puts it brilliantly.

> Now that I have lived almost as many years as had my parents when the violence and controversy over the war in Vietnam divided us, I realize what is obvious but what I never before faced so starkly: As we age, gathering decades on our own account, and if our parents have not died young, we inevitably discover that we lived part of our lives in a world in which our parents never really joined us. I know now that half of my life is still loitering where my parents lived; I honor and perhaps envy what I still manage to perceive as the coherent simplicity of that universe. The other half, the part that moved me away from my origins, contemplates *a world my parents never knew, a world they could hardly understand or sympathize with except by gigantic effort* [italics mine].[4]

It is always this way. My children live in a world where global warming and loss of species is a given, one in which television, and the World Wide Web, and frequent flyer points shape our consciousness.

I grew up in a house where there was no car and no television (an anomaly even then). My vision was closer, therefore, to the ground, to the number of miles I could walk or bicycle. When I tell my children this, they listen interestedly, and with a slight but loving disbelief, as if I were describing my abduction by aliens and eventual return.

In the same way, in churches, at board and committee meetings, we are likely to sit beside people whose experiences place them outside our particular world. It's very hard to get across that gap.

Heilbrun continues, talking about her own children.

Yet whether we feel admiring of our parents, reconciled to them, or still estranged, still teetering near a cliff of anger, *we recognize that we can never meet them in agreement about what we have encountered beyond their experience* [italics mine].[5]

In the end, a kind of denial can overtake us. As long as our elders live, they are a reminder to those younger than themselves of how

one day they too will cease to live completely in the present that surrounds them…because inevitably their children or the young people they know will assign them, as they will assign themselves, to a different, largely abandoned world.[6]

Out of that different world can come wisdom. Those who stand, in Heilbrun's phrase, in "the exact space between generations," can talk about Korea or Vietnam, and the waste of young lives, when we embark on a Peace March. Like the elder women at Tatamagouche, they can show us how to go on after catastrophe, to simply continue with the details of life. They stand as witnesses to our human capacity to survive in faith.

## Our elders do for children what parents cannot

My mother talks about what I was like when I was little. It drives me crazy, but my children listen attentively, alert for signs that they were not the only sometime-rebels in the family.

Of course they weren't.

In the same way, long-time members of the congregation I attend describe with glee the time live animals were used in the Christmas pageant, and the lamb got away and ran bleating to the cathedral across the street, and one of the men caught it just before it burst into the evening service.

They can describe the revered woman who supervised the quilt, that loving community of names that hangs on the chapel wall. Congregational identity is preserved by these stories; we know ourselves to be risk-taking (a *lamb*?) and fun-loving, loving and creative.

In the same way, Native grandmothers sometimes tie a knot in a small sapling when a child is born. Years later, they can take the child and point to a tree with a huge knot, high up, tied in their honor, and tell the story of how they were cherished from the minute they were born.

In fact, Native tradition carries this knowledge intuitively. I was reporting on an assembly of Native people, and a youth was accompanied to the microphone by an older woman. He thanked his grandmother for giving him courage to speak. I discovered later, after I had watched him address the crowd with dignity and skill, with his grandmother's hand on his shoulder, that she was *not* his mother or father's mother at all. She was simply someone of their generation, who loved him.

Churches are full of this kind of love, which we need deeply in a fragmented society. As family therapist Mary Pipher says,

The love of grandparents and grandchildren is often incredibly pure and powerful. I have noticed that most children who have known their grandparents grow up loving older people. They are like kittens who have been gentled and learn to love humans. Children who haven't had that privilege often regard older people as scary or at best irrelevant. They have no idea what they are missing. Unfortunately many things – such as time, divorce and distance – work against what can be an important and beautiful intergenerational bond.[7]

Congregational life can provide that "gentling" for our children, even when their grandparents-by-blood are far away. It is a miracle we can all enjoy. As David said, "Murray walked across the water, and his arms were full of me."

# 11

# The Visionary Congregation
## Building for Others

> Moreover, some women of our group astounded us.
> They were at the tomb early this morning, and when
> they did not find his body there, they came back and
> told us that they had indeed seen a vision of angels
> who said that he was alive.
>
> Luke 24:22–23

**Christopher White**

**Vision:** a mystical, supernatural or prophetic apparition; concept or insight perceived vividly in the imagination; ability to devise or form a far-sighted policy.

**Endurance:** the ability of a person or thing to persevere, hold out, or withstand prolonged strain.

The Emmaus Road is a story of resurrection; it is a story of the shockingly unexpected; it is a story about how our world can change through one encounter; it is a story about vision. The disciples' encounter with the risen Christ transformed not only their hearts, but their very existence. That which was once unimaginable, became the guiding reality of their lives.

This gospel account shows us how God supports us through times of tumultuous and even unwelcome change. Up until Jesus' arrest, the disciples were confident. Finally, events were unfolding as they had expected. But then everything collapsed. They were stunned and left grieving. Only days later, however, new hope revealed itself. In the encounter on the road to Emmaus, the disciples gained a vision of a reality that was different from their current experience.

For too many years, our churches have focused on survival issues. We have looked inwards too often and forgotten our mission to the expanding communities around us. These communities are changing rapidly, becoming more diverse. Populations are shifting quickly to new, fast-growing areas. Though we once saw ourselves as having a mission to plant churches in communities like these, many in the mainline denominations appear to have lost focus and no longer provide the resources so that churches can be built to serve these people. We have become expert at closing churches, but inexpert in strategically planting new ones. But perhaps, like the disciples on the Emmaus Road, a radical re-visioning lies before us.

Of all the experiences that I have had in my 15 years of ministry, by far the hardest, most challenging, and unique, has been the construction of our new church facility. What has made it unique has not been the actual building itself, but the process that has taken us to where we are today. It has been a massive undertaking, one that has called upon all the spiritual, emotional, and financial resources that we have had at our disposal; an undertaking that has both stretched and transformed our congregation into something new.

But why build at all? Does it not seem counterintuitive, if not perverse, to spend large sums of money on a brand-new building in an increasingly secular age? Are there not issues of faithfulness that should come before bricks and mortar?

This is a question that churches have faced for generations. I cannot help but look back to an earlier generation of my family. When my great-grandfather Robert Telfer arrived in Canada as a Methodist missionary in the early part of the last century, he was a pioneer. His family had to adapt to a new climate and culture. They had to learn to homestead in the community of Hazel Bluff, north of Edmonton, Alberta. He was determined, as he rode his horse on his circuit, that a new church be built. His community also held this conviction, because a church building proclaims to the world that God is worshipped in this spot, that here is another power, greater than that wielded by the world. One might ask whether this was a foolish use of scarce resources at the time. After all, family farms were touch and go, there was no money, and times were hard. But still the church was built. People donated their time, their talents, and their money, so that a place of worship could bind their community together. That church, almost 100 years later, still worships each Sunday.

Think what that has meant to the continuity of that community. We are the heirs to that tradition and I cannot help but wonder what my great-grandfather would say were I to tour him through our building site.

Today's churches struggle with the same issues as our forebears did. Southminster Steinhauer United Church, in Edmonton, Alberta, was for decades a church without a building. They prided themselves on being a congregation whose mission could not be contained in walls. But as time went on they discovered something we ourselves found out. Our faith and our mission are shaped by the space we create. In other words, not having a church building, far from freeing them for mission, in reality restricted the mission of that church.

This proved to be the case as well for Trinity Anglican Church in Aurora, Ontario, and St. Peter's Anglican, in Cobourg, Ontario. In both these cases, the congregations have gone through or are preparing for major retrofits costing millions of dollars, because their buildings were preventing them from carrying out their full ministry. Canon Philip Poole informed me that since Trinity Anglican reopened in the spring of 2002, attendance has jumped 40% and 19 new ministries have arisen. Everything from new initiatives in youth ministry, to a community kitchen, to an Amnesty International group, has sprung from the enthusiasm of this new project.

This does not mean that only new buildings allow for contemporary ministry, but rather outdated sanctuary and building space can prevent a congregation from reaching their full potential.

## The "rurban" church?

New buildings do not only spring from large urban or suburban contexts, new rural or "rurban" (neither rural nor urban, both and neither) churches can also emerge. Rev. Sandra Severs has always been linked to building projects. From her first internship in Fort McMurray, Alberta, to Picture Butte and Springbank, Alberta, to West Vancouver, British Columbia, Severs has either arrived at the beginning or the tail end of a building program. Her experience at Picture Butte is particularly instructive.

Located outside of Lethbridge, Picture Butte, with a population of about 1200, is the sugar beet center of southern Alberta. Part of a then four-point charge, it was a church in serious trouble. They were, in Severs' words, "on the slide to nonexistence." They had just sold their building for a dollar to a local seniors group and were meeting for worship in the local library. Their neighbor, Iron Springs, had the opposite problem; their community was in decline, but the congregation was strong. Still, they had a decrepit building, so their future was not bright either. Through their lay leaders, the churches got together and decided to merge the congregations and build a new church in Picture

Butte. These were farmers who were forward thinking and determined not to let their churches die.

This was the situation that Severs faced upon her arrival as a new ordinand. Without any other financial support but their pledges, this resilient congregation not only built a new 200-seat facility, they had it paid for in four years!

## The Westminster story

The congregation I serve, Westminster United, in Whitby, Ontario, had its roots in the post-war baby boom. Initiated by the vision of Kay Moorcroft, who literally went door-to-door to find members, the congregation was formed in 1958. For the first year, they met in a local school. Then a church building was erected on our current site. It was an enormous challenge at the time. Congregants had to sign personal promissory notes guaranteeing the debt. The building they erected was not meant to be a permanent worship space, but rather the church hall, which would in time be supplemented by the larger church, to be built immediately to the east. But the congregation could barely afford the structure they had put up, let alone another building, and so they waited.

The years took their toll and the church that was booming in the late 1950s and early 1960s was in serious decline by the 1970s. By then, the issue was not whether to build a bigger church, but whether the existing congregation would even survive.

The people of Westminster have always had a strong sense of vocation. They felt a genuine call to do something productive with the property they owned and so developed it into a low-rise seniors' complex, providing affordable housing to those on fixed incomes.

By the 1980s, the congregation was growing again. Oshawa Presbytery, which had commissioned a study on the needs of this growing community, approached the congregation and proposed that they sell their building, move north, and build a new church on a larger parcel of land.

This was not something that the church was able to do at that time and so they opted instead to construct a $500,000 addition to their building. It was at this point that I was called to Westminster and watched the church expand and the addition fill up. In the 1990s, we tried a number of options to deal with our growing numbers. We added a second alternative service, then, acting on congregational surveys, created a full second service. This didn't work. Every church has an angel or spirit that helps define it. Ours was a spirit of intentional community shared through worship. Folks were unhappy not seeing one another each week, our Sunday school and music programs were put under strain, and we didn't grow as I thought we would with the new format.

We gave it two years and then looked at other alternatives. We put in a portable classroom for extra Sunday school and meeting space, and used the local school auditorium for major services.

But the same scenario kept unfolding; people couldn't find a place to sit and there was too little parking, so the congregation would shrink to fit the building. New people would come, but others would disappear. In 1998, we formed a working group to explore the possibility of relocating. After hours and weeks of meetings, we concluded that moving was not a viable option. The current church was not worth enough, there was no land close by, and the land we *were* able to find was too expensive. So that, we thought, was that.

Then in September of 2000, our official board met for an all-day retreat to plan future directions for our church. Under the leadership of a very skilled facilitator, our board and trustees began to map out our priorities for the next few years. By the afternoon we realized much to our surprise that our number-one need was a new facility. We had no money, no land, no plan, and a congregation that was sure of one thing

– we weren't moving. Seventeen months later, we broke ground for the new building.

So what happened to so radically change our circumstances?

There are two responses to that question – a religious and a more secular one. The religious or faith-based approach stems out of the Emmaus Road story.

In the same way that the original dreams of the disciples had come to naught, so too, our original hopes had fallen apart. But God had another story written that we could not yet see, a story we had not and in reality *could* not have anticipated. And so while our previous attempts hit nothing but roadblocks, this time every door burst open.

## "Tipping Points"

The more secular response to the question of what happened to change our circumstances comes from Malcolm Gladwell. Gladwell would suggest that our church had experienced "Tipping Points," small moments of change that had catapulted us into the future. In his book *The Tipping Point*, Gladwell shows that social change occurs in huge, spontaneous leaps, as a result of small incremental steps.

His thesis has three major themes. First, there is a contagious element to change that causes it to spread like wildfire. Second, small changes can have big effects. And finally, change happens not gradually, but in one dramatic moment.[1]

Gladwell goes on to say that this process can be broken down into smaller components.

He identifies the first of these as the Law of the Few – it only takes a few people to lead significant change. In a church setting, this requires people who have connections to many members in the congregation, people who possess a deep knowledge of the church and its culture, and finally, people who can convince others of the importance of the proposed change. Gladwell calls these people "connectors, mavens, and persuaders."

Second, the message of change needs to have what he terms "a stickiness factor," which he defines as a "simple way to package information that under the right circumstances can make it irresistible."[2]

While Gladwell uses the example of two children's television programs, *Sesame Street* and *Blues Clues*, I believe Jesus understood this concept extremely well. His use of parable was rich with "stickiness." Those parables have also been described as ticking time bombs that would explode in people's lives. They would listen to his stories about prodigal sons and good Samaritans and realize that he was talking about *them* and *their* lives; then an explosion of realization would hit them. Even today, people who have no church context have heard the phrase "the Good Samaritan" and have an understanding, however incomplete, of its meaning. The stories of Jesus have a message that resonates in people's lives. Likewise, the church is replete with stickiness.

The third component is the power of context. By this, Gladwell means that small changes in the immediate context can have tremendous results. The example he uses is the "broken window theory" of crime. This theory posits that crime arises out of disorder. So if streets and subways are allowed to decay, crime grows in these locales. New York City cleaned up the graffiti on its subways – i.e., attended to its "broken windows" – and the crime rate fell.

In a church setting it would work like this: Say you have a congregation that is unskilled in welcoming people. Guests arrive and depart never having been spoken to warmly. Stagnation sets in. The congregation does not feel welcoming. So you institute a special congregational-wide welcoming program. People are identified as they walk in the church; they are spoken to at coffee time; a card is sent to them and maybe a small souvenir of their time with you. Results? The atmosphere changes. Long-time people become more animated, more enthusiastic, and the church starts to grow again. Why? Not because of huge changes, but because people receive a smile and a word of welcome on Sunday morning.

So what were the Tipping Points for some of the congregations I mentioned earlier? According to Peter Walker, Rector of St. Peter's Anglican, the church that underwent the retrofits, there were a variety. First, he built a staff team that was able to reach each group in the church. They began children's liturgies that actively involved the children in worship. When the children feel involved and important, they want to attend, and so do their parents. Peter also credits the Alpha program with having a positive impact on the church's growth. Finally, they began a Parish Nursing program, which enriched the church's ministry.

For Southminster Steinhauer, the congregation that had intentionally gone without a building for decades, the Tipping Point occurred during a visioning exercise in 1992. According to Rev. Bob Hetherington, that's when they realized they needed a space that was not under the control of others. They felt strongly that real outreach into the community required a defined place.

For us at Westminster, first there was the retreat that identified the need. At the same time, just under three acres of land became available one kilometer north of our current location. Owned by the Anglican Church and designated as a church site, the Anglicans did not want to sell it to a developer; they wanted a church to be built on the property. So they instructed their broker to approach churches until they found a buyer. And there we were! For us, it was a perfect location within our current catchment area, but far enough north to access the new homes being built. After much discussion, the Anglicans offered the property to us at below market value and we had the beginnings of a plan. We went from strength to strength. The property was sold to us with the assistance of our presbytery's Church Extension Council, and we had a site. A buyer who hadn't been in the market two years previously, approached us about the current building. These two events gave us a focus and made the dream possible.

## What's involved

When I review the tasks that we had to accomplish together to make the new building a reality, I feel almost overwhelmed. Although every situation is different and will dictate its own set of requirements, the following list of things that Westminster undertook will provide a good overview of what's involved.

1) Build consensus among the congregation that a move is the right thing to do.
2) Find and buy land.
3) Hire a consultant to survey the congregation and determine what they need from the building.
4) Create a rough budget.
5) Create and staff a Building and Design Team, Stewardship Team, and a Ministry and Outreach Team.
6) Find a project manager.
7) Obtain the approval(s) of your presbytery or other governing body.
8) Hire an architect.
9) Hire a builder.
10) Interview and hire a stewardship consultant for a capital campaign.
11) Run a capital stewardship campaign.
12) Obtain municipal approvals.
13) Run a focus group for users outside church.
14) Host an open community meeting and invite all new neighbors to see the plans.

15) Find financing.
16) Put together a detailed budget.
17) Get approval of congregation/presbytery for building design and detailed budget.
18) Change design after full congregational consultation.
19) List old building for sale, find a buyer, and negotiate sale agreement.
20) Submit architect's design to National Architectural Committee.
21) Adjust design after report from National Architectural Committee.
22) Find a volunteer to coordinate congregational workers on the building site.
23) Find volunteers.
24) Find a special event fund-raising coordinator.
25) Find a lawyer.
26) Choose furnishings and colors for exterior and interior.
27) Engage in pews versus chairs debate.
28) Help organize retreats on worship, outreach, Christian education.

### For the pastor specifically

29) Juggle 45 balls in the air at the same time, while preaching, visiting the sick, and doing the other parts of your job.
30) Realize that your job is now different.
31) Pray that everyone else realizes it.
32) Meet daily with your Ministry and Personnel Committee.

All right, the last bit was a small attempt at humor, but it was true nonetheless. I also omitted some tasks that were very specific to Westminster – such as subdividing the old property so that we could keep the retirement apartments. No doubt, each congregation will have its own set of unique challenges.

## Keys to success

What made this project a success for Westminster was quite simply the overwhelming congregational support it received – 85% in favor of buying the land and 98% in favor of the final project. Many elements contributed to this result, but one of the most significant factors was the support of our founders, that generation of people who had built our existing building. It was our elders who saw the need and who realized the sacrifice and effort involved.

Another key factor was the longevity of my ministry. Over the last decade we had developed a level of deep trust. That continuity was critical.

We also kept the congregation informed and hired a consultant to survey the whole church about this project. Thus, everyone had input and the project was designed around the needs of the whole church.

One central element that came out of the consultation process was the clearly stated need to *not* build a multi-purpose sanctuary. For this group, a sanctuary was for worship, concerts, speaking engagements, but not for ball hockey or basketball. The congregation had a very clear understanding of what sacred space meant to them. I recognize that different churches have their own definition that arises out of their experience and context. In another place, another decision could have been reached. While this decision flew in the face of much current literature, it was an important signal that we were listening to people's needs and would adapt our design to fit our particular set of circumstances. When the consultation was complete, the result was a 19,000 sq. ft. building that can seat close to 500 in the main sanctuary, and another 200 on chairs in the narthex. We built a gym/common room, a lounge/library, a music room, Christian education space designed around the rotation model of church school, a dedicated computer room, a dedicated youth room, and plenty of office space, including storage areas – for a cost of $3 million.

## Peaks and pitfalls

From her own experience at Picture Butte, Sandra Severs believes that leaders building churches need a few key characteristics. First, they need the ability not to be overwhelmed by anxiety – their own or the natural anxiety of others. Second, they must function as the chief cheerleader, keep people calm, and be prepared to pay a heavy physical (and I would add spiritual) price in exhaustion by the time the building opens.

In addition to these, I would add that clergy and congregations who are considering new church development need to be ready for the following realities. The project will go well and the project will go wrong, often within the same hour, and you will have to cope with a succession of emotional highs and lows. Finances will be a problem; both the building fund and the operating fund will face significant challenges. People may divert money from their operating donations to the building fund, which will put pressure on your operating fund. Constructing a building or retrofitting an old one is a new venture and many new ventures lose money at first. When I arrived at Westminster, at the tail end of their earlier building program, there was a large operating deficit and a building debt. Within five years, they eliminated the building debt and within two years the operating fund was back in the black.

All new buildings create conflict. People will leave because of the project – people you are close to. It hurts. Inevitably, in the area of pastoral care, somebody will fall through the cracks. You can put together the best team imaginable and it will still happen. New church development puts a whole new layer of responsibility onto clergy and other parts of their work will pay a price.

The people involved in the project are under significant stress. Wisdom will not always be used in their (or your) words. A significant amount of time will be invested soothing bruised feelings that arise from words spoken in haste.

For clergy, it is key that your vision be at least six months ahead of where the project is currently situated. Your job is to keep the vision before the people and to assemble the necessary teams for the next tasks.

Change is difficult; massive change creates pressure. But so does small change. Some issue that you may consider very minor, like an alteration in the order of worship, can push somebody else to the wall. I once heard what I hope was an apocryphal story about a minister who was in a meeting to select the color for the new sanctuary. When the choice was announced, the minister resigned on the spot. I used to laugh at that story, but not anymore.

According to Pastor Darren Gavin of Trinity Pentecostal, in Oshawa, Ontario, once you are in your new church prepare for a backlash. People suddenly realize that the building does not in and of itself have magical powers. The people are the same and the issues are the same issues and both remain to be dealt with.

But do not be discouraged! The building of a new church is an act of supreme faith – faith in God and faith in each other. The result of the work and the sacrifice is the creation of a new place to worship God. It means having a new center of outreach and compassion in the community, a new place for youth and seniors, and new opportunities to serve God.

In my region alone, there has been $15 million in new church construction in the past year and a half, which speaks volumes about the growing need for new churches.

## Financial assistance and vision

Not surprisingly, one of the most pressing problems facing congregations like ours is a lack of financial assistance from our national church. As Vince Alfano, head of the Toronto United Church Council puts it, "We have no national strategy for new church development." In the

United Church of Canada, new church development comes under the authority of the presbytery, not the conference or the national church. As a result, there is no national vision in our denomination for new church developments. There is not enough significant money available for capital projects.

The consequences of this failure have been dire. While other denominations such as the Pentecostal churches deliberately plant new ministries into high growth areas, the United Church leaves this in the hands of local congregations that may have neither the skill nor the ability to do this work.

Reginald Bibby, in his analysis of the mainline church, identifies this Achilles heel when he writes,

> One important factor I think has been very much underplayed, however, was suggested to me a few years back by the Moderator at the time, Marion Best. To the extent Mainliners did not give high priority in the 1970s and 1980s to aggressively establishing new congregations, particularly in new suburbs, they missed out on the opportunity and the need to minister to young families who already identified with them. The number of United Church congregations, for example, dropped from 4,355 in 1973 to 4,112 by 1990… Because adequate numbers of new Mainline churches had not been created, the flow of younger active affiliates was reduced and dying members were not replaced with younger ones.[3]

Alfano believes that the United Church has allowed itself to become distracted from one of its key missions over the past 20 years, and thus has lost a precious opportunity to reach out to new communities. His frustration has also been with theological colleges, which in his view have resisted placing church development as a priority in their curriculum.

My own experience would echo that. The irony is that I have spent my entire ministry involved in church development, either initiating or completing building programs. I have done this without any resources or training. Mainline Canadian literature on this is, to say the least, thin on the ground. Further, any recommendations on this issue seem to die at the General Council level, abandoning congregations and their pastors to do it themselves, hopefully in partnerships with visionary presbyteries.

John Perigoe of the national church echoes this frustration. Under our current structure everything except ordination rests on the presbytery, an organization that by its very nature is ill-equipped with either resources or staff to provide leadership in this area. There are significant exceptions to the rule. Oshawa Presbytery (among others) has supported and, through its Church Extension Council, helped to fund the building of two new churches in our region alone.

But sadly, there is so much more to be done.

John has been instrumental in restarting a new capital assistance program for church development and is to be commended for this. But the $400,000 per year, per project – which must be repaid as quickly as possible and upon which interest is charged – is a drop in the bucket of our denomination's true needs. (One could also ask why these monies must be repaid, when money given by the Mission and Service fund to development projects doesn't have to be.)

The United Church as a whole consistently gets in its own way in areas of new church development. We confuse faithfulness with fear and institutional lethargy. If we believe that the mainline church has a vital message to our world, then we should be investing five times the amount of money that we currently set aside. Our nation is undergoing a profound demographic and geographic shift. If we fail to place new church communities in growing areas, then I would argue we have failed the test of faith. Instead of going on to Jerusalem, we choose to stay in Emmaus, afraid to move.

Evangelical congregations are springing up in new buildings, industrial malls, and even in movie theatres. Are we in these same places? Should not our message be as significant to the human story as theirs?

We need innovative conversations to happen among all the mainline churches. How can we create new places of worship? Is the recent shared Jewish/United Church congregation in Kitchener, Ontario, the model of the future? Or is the Springdale Mission, in Brampton, Ontario, the way we should move? Led by Rev. Jim Cairney, the Springdale Mission purchased a small mall from a developer and holds its worship services in the building's atrium. In Courtice, Ontario, Faith United opened their building a year ago. An amalgamation of a declining inner-city church, St. Andrew's, and a rural church, Courtice, this new church has brought life not only to Faith United, but has spurred redevelopment and new ministries in the remaining downtown church in Oshawa, Simcoe Street United. Instead of two dying churches, there are now two vibrant communities of faith. It is vision like this that we need to embrace.

Are we being called to share buildings and pool resources with other denominations, or with other faiths?

I strongly believe that there is no universal model, simply local structures and concepts that emerge to fit particular situations and contexts. But questions remain. How do we train for, support, and fund these new ministries? How do we develop skilled leadership that combines the pastoral and the prophetic, and that creates the imagination needed to envision new possibilities? How do we save the staff involved from exhaustion and burnout? These are not easy questions. There *are* no easy answers. But they are critical to our future.

**12**

# The Contemplative Congregation
## Walking with the Spirit

Then their eyes were opened, and they recognized him;
and he vanished from their sight.
They said to each other, "Were not our hearts
burning within us...?"
Luke 24:31–32

**Donna Sinclair**

Silence:   1. the absence of sound or noise; stillness.
   2. the state or quality of being or keeping still
   and silent.
   3. a period of time without speech.

The inner life is like this: the instant we recognize something essential, something important, it vanishes from our sight. We begin to chatter, needing to talk to one another. That is an understandable impulse.

But congregations need to provide a space within themselves for those whose first impulse is to keep silence. When something significant happens, they sit still and meditate on what this mystery means. Reading this passage, one wonders if Jesus vanished at the moment of recognition, like a rock star fearful of publicity, because he simply didn't want to face the chatter.

"We need to find God, and [God] cannot be found in noise and restlessness," says Mother Teresa. "God is the friend of silence. See how nature – trees, flowers, grass – grows in silence; see the stars, the moon and the sun, how they move in silence... We need silence to be able to touch souls."[1]

Congregations need to be able to provide this gentle space, especially for those who have come in from the secular world, searching; for those who are unused to the purposeful, cheerful bustle of congregational life. Here's a story of my own, about someone who attends no church, but has much to teach us about spirituality.

## Anam Cara

The Celtic concept of the soul friend entered my house last year with a phone call. A woman was looking for someone to do dream work with – we had held a dream group in our congregation for many years – and thought I might know something about it. We talked for some time and finally decided that I would be her *anam cara* – in Gaelic, "soul friend" – for a year. I would simply listen to her dreams and try to see what she was not seeing in them. I would tell her what I see behind her blind spot. In return, I would be free to attend as many classes at her yoga studio as I wished.

Neither of us is young, nor are we unskilled. She is a therapist, and I have led dream groups for many years.

But this is different from leading dream groups or doing therapy. We feel obliged to one another. I, who can scarcely cope with any kind of exercise program except gardening, feel I need to be (as her friend) at yoga class. She researches dreams, makes copious notes, and brings them to me. I try to listen to what she, and they, are saying.

Sometimes I can hear the story of a Jacob or a Lazarus whispering through her dreams, even though she has little "church" background. Out of years of Bible study, I can describe to her the story evoked by her dreams. Last week, for example, she brought me this odd dream about the push-pins that hold up notices on her bulletin board at the studio.

> Imagine something that looks like a brooch, perhaps three to four inches large. Now imagine that something looks like angel wings but you aren't sure until you draw back the one on the right, and you see this is a little angel/fairy. In fact, three angels/fairies manifest, as the one collapsed wing is lifted up and back. It's as if they were in a semi-circle with the tiniest one at the center.

I could only laugh, because, nestled on the end of the pin, were three angels. At a time when she was wondering about the wisdom of some effort in her life, I could tell her that the ancient question of the scholastics – how many angels can dance on the head of a pin? – was being answered in her simple studio. Three. She was being assured that she was wise, which I knew already, but she didn't. And God, the Trinity, was with her, which I thought I knew already – but she didn't.

## The church needs mystery and mysticism

Congregations need to be about this exactly, this careful listening to each other. And they very often are. It is delightful. We learn from each other and are calm, searching each other's souls. This is *anam cara*, the friendship between two people that allows them to read each other's hearts – oh yes, haltingly, and only from time to time – but still, more and better than usual.

It happens in women's groups. Some cherish the kind of friendship that develops through shared labor, for example. "Quilting," as United Church Women member and senator Joan Cook says, "quilting and between the stitches getting our lives straightened out."

This skilled listening happens in theatre groups, in the altar guild and, very often, in the choir. It happens in Bible study – in fact, whenever and wherever people trust each other and find silence together. Then it's "like a fire burning within us," as we recognize the presence of Christ.

This is a power for which the world is starved, but doesn't know how to name. You can only see the yearning for it – at Christmas Eve, for instance, in the delight of normally non-attending adults, caught by the candles and music. They have gone further into mystery than they usually go. They are brought to the presence of God, whether they believe in precisely this kind of God, or not.

## How do we do this?

One way congregations can get in touch with the depth of mystery within is through a dream group. For many years our congregation cherished one. About 30 to 40 people met once a month in the church parlor. It continues still, in one form or another, sometimes meeting at church, sometimes in homes. This is what we did.

We began with people who had an interest in dreams, or at least, in the inner life. One or two psychologists were often there; a wise woman who studied astrology always came; and there were teachers and other learners. Two of us (my spouse and I) had attended a week-long seminar called "Dreams as God's Forgotten Language" at Five Oaks, one of our denomination's education and retreat centers. While none of us was an expert, most knew the importance of searching the inner life.

We all shared what knowledge we had. Jim and I did our best to reproduce lectures we had heard at Five Oaks, and – also important – described what we had learned from studying our own dreams, and reading. We started a little library and even got some funding from the congregation to buy more books on dream theory to pass around.

Each week (we met every fourth Friday evening) we would begin all together, as a large group, tucked in a large comfortable circle, gathering information and sharing knowledge and insights from the month. We often talked about the relationship between the Bible and dreams; and about the value of our hymns (wonderful repositories of symbols) as a kind of living dictionary that could unlock dream messages.

Often someone would offer a dream for the whole group's learning. Here's an example, from one dreamer:

I was in a tall apartment building, with all the windows sealed tightly. A strong wind was battering it, and it was swaying back and forth.

Immediately, one of the group mentioned the hymn *I Feel the Winds of God*. That gave us a clue. Perhaps this mighty wind in the dream was God, trying to get in. Then we offered, respectfully, associations and questions, wondering how a person might be like a tall apartment building, what wind might need to flow, and more.

Moving away from that dream, someone might offer some gleanings from a new book they had read; others would present a question and the group would pool its expertise to try to answer.

Then we would break into small groups, about four or five people in each one, and vanish in different directions, some to the chapel and some to staff offices, like so many interested church mice. Chairs would be pulled into a circle, and the really hard work, the "soul work" of the evening, would begin. Each member of the little group would take their turn telling a dream. The other three or four would listen intently, with their hearts as much as with their heads, saying nothing until the dream was told. Then they would approach the dream in various ways.

Sometimes they would amplify it. They would say "that dream figure [or object] makes me think of…" and then they would call up all the literary or biblical associations they could think of, to lend richness to the possibility of the dream.

Sometimes they would look for puns, which dreams love dearly.

Sometimes they would simply ask questions. When a woman dreamed of a wrought iron balcony, they asked: "How are you like iron? What is your strength right now?"

They would watch carefully for certain common dream themes. If the dreamer was flying, they would wonder aloud if he or she might be having difficulty being grounded, or simply flying free. If there was smoke or fire, they might ask if there was anger smoldering. If there was rain, they might ask if new growth was being watered by tears.

They would elicit events from the day before the dream, listening for the shift in voice that signaled the dream was about this or that piece of unfinished business.

They never pretended to be experts, because they weren't. They were simply soul friends, respectful listeners, accompaniers into the world of the spirit.

And there were certain rules and assurances they followed, to safeguard them on their way.

1. The dreamer always owns her or his dream. Nobody else can say what it means. Even if you think you know what it means, don't say it, just ask questions. The dreamer may not be ready to hear your interpretation yet, even if it *is* correct. The dreamer will come to the dream as he or she is ready.

2. A dream will not hurt you. (That's partly why it is important not to "tell" the interpretation.) The dream comes from God, part of the language God once used with Jacob and Joseph and others.

3. Even if a meaning or a message is not found in the dream, still the dream – and the dreamer – has been honored, healed in a way, by the telling and the listening, the speaking out of one's soul to others who wait silently and do their very best to hear.

4. Our group always tried to make sure there was an elder in each smaller group: for example, a wise person who had the authority to stop anyone from treading accidentally on someone's dream. "The dream belongs to the dreamer…" they might say gently to an overzealous participant.

We had a wonderful time. People attended as their schedules and needs allowed; there was no obligation to be present. They brought their friends, and other gifts: their dream books, sometimes filled with drawings; their reading, which grew more and more expert as months went by; their laughter, because dreams can be extremely funny; and sometimes, their tears.

Our dream group strengthened the congregation. Although all 30 or 40 people weren't members, most were. They became close to one another, trusting one another more. And, out of the respect the dreams demanded, they developed the habit of speaking respectfully to one another. It was a form of outreach too; a way for those whose experience of church had not been kind to know that it is not always thus.

Most of all, it answered the yearning for mystery that lies within each person today. I am sure of this. A few times, in the fall, we went away to a fishing lodge and spent the weekend walking in the fiery maple woods, poking at a smoky fire, and talking about dreams. I felt, at those times, that the spirit of God was very near. We prayed together and shared communion, and our hearts were full of each other and the dreams.

## Writers' groups

There are other ways to get at this mystery. A writers' group, for instance, could meet in a church. They might want to include prayers and hymns in the pieces they bring to read to one another. They might want to write a new hymn for a certain Sunday in the liturgical year, fitting it to the theme of worship. And they might discover (just as in a dream group) that by listening to one another as soul friends, by meeting together over a long period of time, and by hearing each other's poems and prayers, they become beautiful to one another.

Sometimes when I work with writers' groups, I ask each person to bring her or his favorite work, and we sit in a circle and read aloud in turns. We do not comment or critique, we just listen carefully and go on to the next.

It has the same effect, I find, an evening with a dream group. Somehow, in the careful listening, and the moment of silence that follows each person's work, there is a descent into the soul. We become, just for that moment, each other's *anam cara*. We become church to one another.

## Mystery is what the church does

There is more to this searching after mystery, and it is important. This is the business (or part of it) of church: to seek out and support any enterprise that stills the noise so that our soul can heal.

And it is not only sound that is noisy in North American mainstream culture. We have noisy light, too, artificial street-light that stops us from seeing the stars and that takes away both the mystery of night and the enchantment of the slowly breaking dawn.

But congregations have a particular gift for light. We have a history of candles. As John O'Donohue says,

The Celtic mind adored the light. This is one of the reasons Celtic spirituality is emerging as a new constellation in our times. We are lonely and lost in our hungry transparency. We desperately need a new and gentle light where the soul can shelter and reveal its ancient belonging. We need a light that has retained its kinship with the darkness.[2]

This gentle light is often found in church. Small children stretch on tiptoe to light the candle that, in some congregations, signals a new grandchild, or a baptism about to take place. Or Advent. Or Christmas. Or the memory of someone who has died.

All eyes focus on the tiny candle. It is a light as far from an orange streetlight or a neon sign as we can imagine. Perhaps this focus will heal eyes dulled by neon, and ears taught not to hear by snowmobiles and muscle cars and the never-ending grind of leaf blowers, snow blowers, heavy lawn mowers, air conditioning units, and car alarms.

If the church has this quiet light, even once in a while, even just on Christmas Eve, perhaps people will be able to remember what it looks like and how there is warm mystery in darkness, and how the silence sounds.

Congregations need to look at what they do in what they are pleased to call "retreats." Retreats should not always be about church business, or the search for a new program or technique. Many congregations sponsor annual canoe trips, where – sitting in a tent on a rainy day, perhaps, watching the light dim – one can discover again what O'Donohue means by "gentle light."

But congregations don't always have to go away. At Bible study and worship, dream group or prayer circle, evensong and Taizé-style worship, churches can create caves of quiet for those hungry for it.

This is mystery. The world needs it.

## Conclusion

The two disciples walked and talked with Jesus for a long time without seeing that the Christ was with them. This is precisely the story of the church in our time. In these chapters, I have described nothing new. Everything in them is a description of the work that has been done by congregations for years. Centuries, really. It is time we recognized who is with us.

We somehow believe these days that we are nothing, that the work we do as churches counts for little. We have forgotten who we are. What we do is everything.

Congregations equip their members to discern good from evil, offering Bible study and preaching and prayers for that purpose. They bring visitors from beyond their own borders (borders of culture or class, of politics or geography) and invite those visitors to speak about *their* world. In the process, congregations are often set on fire with a passion for justice – something television and newspapers, with all their gifts, cannot do.

Healing occurs over dirty dishes in congregations, and hospitality emerges in the form of quiet listening from the most unlikely sources. True, though unspoken, communion is celebrated at coffee breaks and over potluck suppers in every corner of the building.

To us, as to the disciples, the story must by now be clear. The Christ is among us. We should not be afraid. We should only be who we are – holding up what courage and obedience, compassion and confidence, hospitality and generativity, we can muster. Jesus (unseen, perhaps, as elusive to our physical vision as he was to Cleopas and the other disciple) is among us.

The Emmaus Road is the one we all walk, never alone. Rejoice, then, for Christ is risen.

# Epilogue

I've sat in the same congregation for many years, and seen some miracles there. An angry, awkward child loved into gentleness by a patient community. A shy adult, who somehow finds the courage to step forward to say a prayer, or sing in the choir.

I've seen people blessed and sent to places in the Two-thirds World, to study and work. They come home transformed. Over and over, I have seen hearts melted, eyes opened, voices discovered. Normally, serious grownups teach Sunday school and find the spirit of a child. In the fire of candlelight, the phrase of a song, cynical people rediscover mystery and are startled by their tears.

These miracles occur all over this country. They are why the church survives. Jesus is with us. He is talking politics, and breaking bread, and being held, fragile, in the minister's arms to be baptized. Sometimes we recognize him – more often we don't. But he is here, alive in those moments when we have courage and tenderness in the face of fear and loss.

We've been trying to say – all through these pages – that Emmaus is here and now. It needs no Powerpoint presentation (although it does not vanish if you use one). It doesn't even require great leadership, efficient buildings, great sound systems, a growing population, or a revival (although those things are wonderful, to be sure). It just takes two or three called disciples, gathered together.

And a journey and a meal shared in hospitality.

All the rest is miracle.

Donna Sinclair

It's a rainy June day in Toronto. I am sitting with Rev. Rob Oliphant in a restaurant on Yonge Street having just toured his church's construction site. Oliphant is part of the pastoral team of Eglinton-St. George's, a newly merged downtown congregation. The Eglinton site was sold for condominiums, and the St. George's site is undergoing an exciting transformation into a 21st-century facility.

Oliphant is speaking to me about an experience he had at Glide Memorial, in San Francisco. Glide is located in the Tenderloin district, one of that city's toughest and most dangerous areas. The church seats over 800 and there was a line-up to get in for the service. The preacher, Cecil Williams, led a low-tech worship experience, with a powerful African-American choir. The service, the music, and the sermon were so deeply profound, that they moved Oliphant to tears. Like John Wesley before him, his heart was strangely warmed. He told me that he finally understood the meaning of Jesus' life, death, and resurrection, and he wept. In that church that was filled with the rich, the poor, the drug addicted, and the prostitute, Oliphant had a profound experience of God, and it changed him. Like those on the Emmaus Road, it was the *encounter* that transformed him.

Oliphant believes that the churches also need to experience this encounter. He drew for me the Wesleyan Quadilateral:

**Scripture**          **Reason**

**Tradition**          **Experience**

"The church," he told me, "has gone so far to the reason side that we are out of balance; we are losing our capacity to appreciate God's glory, God's awe, and we have eliminated the sense of mystery."

Sadly, I think he's right. But there are signs that we are moving in a new direction. The Ancient Future movement pioneered by Robert Webber mixes all our different strands together – mystery, sacrament, wonder, and ancient styles of worship and music – in contemporary formats, using technology as servant not savior.

I believe it is a mistake to think that there is only one path we can follow. Instead, each congregation needs to find its own path, not in an anxious way, but embracing what's best for them, right now. If your church wants to try the new and the innovative, do so. If you wish to stay with the tried and the loved, do so. If you want to do both, experiment with combinations of jazz, drama, the visual, praise music, Taizé, and the traditional. We should not be afraid to attempt all sorts of things as we travel down our own Emmaus Roads. Although we may not at times recognize him, Jesus is walking beside us. So let us hear the word, welcome the stranger, build community, minister with our youth, and reach out to new communities, all the while recognizing and transforming the times in which we live.

This is the 300th anniversary of John Wesley's birth. As we move into the new century, let us remember how just a few people acting with compassion, commitment, and unshakeable faith, transformed their world and ours. If it happened then, why not now? If it happened to them, why not to us?

Christopher White

# Endnotes

## Introduction

1. Reginald Bibby, *Restless Gods: The Renaissance of Religion in Canada* (Stoddart, 2002), p. 77.
2. Ibid., p. 76.
3. Ibid., p. 7.

## Chapter 1

1. Thomas Homer Dixon, *The Ingenuity Gap* (New York: Vintage Books, 2002), p. 34.
2. Bjorn Lomberg, *The Skeptical Environmentalist: Measuring the Real State of the World* (Cambridge, UK: Cambridge University Press, 1998), p. 328.
3. Brian McLaren in an e-mail conversation, June 12, 2002.
4. Leonard Sweet, *AquaChurch: Essential Leadership Arts for Piloting Your Church in Today's Fluid Culture* (Loveland, CO: Group Publishing, 1999), p. 137.
5. Brian McLaren, *The Church on the Other Side: Doing Ministry in the Postmodern Matrix* (Grand Rapids: Zondervan, 2000), p. 59.
6. Philip Jenkins, *The Next Christendom: The Coming of Global Christianity* (New York: Oxford University Press, 2002), p. 5.
7. Ibid., p. 9.
8. Herbert O'Driscoll, from a conversation.
9. McLaren, *The Church on the Other Side*, p. 164.
10. Ibid., p. 167.
11. Gilbert Adair, *Sunday Times Books*, April 21, 1991.
12. Vinay Menon, in *The Toronto Star*, August 3, 2002, H6.
13. Ibid.
14. Ibid.
15. Kennon Callahan, *The Future That Has Come: The Possibilities for Reaching and Growing the Grassroots* (San Francisco: Jossey-Bass, 2002), pp. 193–194.
16. Samuel P. Huntingdon, *The Clash of Civilizations and the Remaking of World Order* (New York: Simon and Schuster, 1996), p. 321.

## Chapter 2

1   Daniel Goleman, Richard Boyatzis, and Annie McKee, *Primal Leadership: Realizing the Power of Emotional Intelligence* (Boston: Harvard Business School Press, 2002), p. 202.

## Chapter 3

1   Jenkins, *The Next Christendom*, p. 214.
2   Bruce Feiler, *Abraham: A Journey to the Heart of Three Faiths* (New York: William Morrow, 2002), p. 203.
3   Ibid., pp. 203–204.
4   Jonathan Sacks, *The Dignity of Difference: How to Avoid the Clash of Civilizations* (London: Continuum, 2002), pp. 17–18.
5   Ibid., pp. 7, 12.
6   Ibid., pp. 53, 59.
7   William Willimon, "Answering Pilate: Truth and the Postliberal Church," at www.religion-online.org
8   Ibid.
9   Philip Kenneson, "The Alleged Incorrigibility of Postliberal Theology," in *The Nature of Confession: Evangelicals & Postliberals in Conversation*, Timothy Phillips, Dennis Okholm, eds. (Downers Grove, IL: InterVarsity Press, 1996), p. 94.

## Chapter 4

1   Tracy Sinclair, personal notes from Tuesday, September 12, 2000.
2   Henri Nouwen, *Gracias: A Latin American Journal* (New York: Harper & Row, 1983), p. 136.
3   Ibid., p. 137.
4   Ursula Franklin, quoted by Michael Valpy in "The Public Good," in *The Globe and Mail*, January 19, 2002, p. F6.
5   John Dominic Crossan, *The Historical Jesus: The Life and Death of a Mediterranean Jewish Peasant* (San Francisco: HarperSanFrancisco, 1991), p. xii.
6   Ibid., p. xiii.
7   Ibid.

# Chapter 5

1   Doug Mackay, "Community Comes in Threes," in *The United Church Observer*, November, 2002, p. 37.
2   Robert Putnam, *Bowling Alone: The Collapse and Revival of American Community* (New York: Simon and Schuster, 2000), p. 19.
3   Ibid., p. 231.
4   John Locke, *Why We Don't Talk To Each Other Anymore: The De-voicing of Society* (New York: Simon and Schuster, 1998), p. 157.
5   Ibid., p. 158
6   From www.conversationcafe.org
7   Randy Frazee, *The Connecting Church: Beyond Small Groups to Authentic Community* (Grand Rapids: Zondervan, 2001), p. 21.
8   Ibid., p. 109.
9   Ibid., p. 179.
10  Putnam, *Bowling Alone,* pp. 393–394.
11  Mardi Tindal, "Common Life," from *Women's Concerns*, April 2002.

# Chapter 6

1   Henri J. M. Nouwen, *Reaching Out: Three Movements of the Spiritual Life* (NY: Doubleday, 1966), p. 74.
2   Ibid.
3   "Peace Falls into Darkness," music and English text by Ralph Johnston, 1997.
4   Edwin H. Friedman, *Generation to Generation: Family Process in Church and Synagogue* (New York: The Guilford Press, 1985), p. 223.
5   Ibid.
6   Ibid., p. 229.
7   Ibid.
8   Donna Sinclair, "Brave New Worship," in *The United Church Observer*, September 2002, p. 27.
9   Ian Bradley, *Celtic Christian Communities: Live the Tradition* (Kelowna, BC: Northstone Publishing, 2001), p. 235.
10  "Solidarity with Victims of Climate Change: Reflections on the World Council of Churches' response to Climate Change," by the World Council of Churches (Justice, Peace and Creation), January 2002, p. 15.

## Chapter 7

1   Mark Devries, *Family-Based Youth Ministry: Reaching the Been-There, Done-That Generation* (Downers Grove, IL: InterVarsity Press, 1994), p. 66.
2   Ibid., p. 55.
3   Ibid., p. 177.
4   Kenda Creasy Dean and Ron Foster, *The Godbearing Life: The Art of Soul Tending for Youth Ministry* (Nashville: Upper Room Books, 1998), p. 27.

## Chapter 8

1   Madeleine L'Engle, *Walking on Water: Reflections on Faith and Art* (New York: Bantam, 1980), p. 55.
2   Dawn Vaneyk, in a letter dated February 23, 2000.
3   Bob Haverluck, from the jacket notes for the tape set *Glory to God in the Lowest: Arguments for a New Theology of Culture from the Dragonfly Café* (Winter Thaw Ink).
4   L'Engle, *Walking on Water*, p. 54.

## Chapter 9

1   www.kerygma.com/mainpages/theology.htm
2   Nicky Gumbel, *What about Other Religions?* (Eastbourne, UK: Kingsway Publications, 1994), pp. 8, 11, 15.
3   Adapted from D. H. Brundage and D. MacKeracher, *Adult Learning Principles and Their Application to Program Planning* (Toronto: Ministry of Education, 1980).
4   Malcolm S. Knowles, Elwood F. Holton III, and Richard A. Swanson, *The Adult Learner: The Definitive Classic in Adult Education and Human Resource Development* (Houston: Gulf Publishing, 1998), pp. 64–69.
5   Ibid., p. 183.

## Chapter 10

1   From "Dr. Borg's Life Cycle," in *Adulthood*, Erik Erickson, editor (Norton, NY, 1978), p. 7.
2   Ibid., p. 26.
3   Letter from a friend, dated April 28, 2002.
4   Carolyn G. Heilbrun, *The Last Gift of Time: Life Beyond Sixty* (New York: The Dial Press, 1997), p. 188.
5   Ibid., p. 189.

6    Ibid.
7    Mary Pipher, *The Shelter of Each Other: Rebuilding Our Families* (New York: Ballantine Books, 1997) p. 242.

## Chapter 11

1    Malcolm Gladwell, *The Tipping Point: How Little Things Can Make a Big Difference* (New York: Little Brown & Company, 2000), adapted from chapter 1.
2    Ibid., p. 132.
3    Reginald Bibby, *Restless Gods: The Renaissance of Religion in Canada* (Toronto, Stoddart, 2002), p. 21.

## Chapter 12

1    Mother Teresa, from *The Columbia Dictionary of Quotations*, Columbia Univesity Press, 1996-97 edition), *Microsoft Bookshelf CD Rom.*
2    John O'Donohue, *Anam Cara: A Book of Celtic Wisdom* (New York: HarperCollins, 1997), p. 4.

## Also by
## Donna Sinclair and Christopher White

**JACOB'S BLESSING**
*Dreams, Hopes, & Visions for the Church*
A hopeful and inspirational vision of the future of the church. Video and
study guide also available.
ISBN 1-55145-381-9


## If you enjoyed this book you may also enjoy these other
## books from Wood Lake Books and Northstone Publishing

**DYING CHURCH, LIVING GOD**
*A Call to Begin Again*
CHUCK MEYER
Acknowledgement of the death of the church and the inevitable
resurrection is both the premise and the promise of this provocative,
enlightening book.
ISBN 1-896836-39-9


**FUTURE FAITH CHURCHES**
*Reconnecting with the Power of the Gospel*
*for the 21st Century*
DON POSTERSKI & GARY NELSON
Churches showing the way into the next millennium.
ISBN 1-55145-098-4


**THERE'S GOT TO BE MORE!**
*Connecting Churches and Canadians*
REGINALD BIBBY
Explores how churches can reach new people.
ISBN 1-55145-048-8

**SPIRITSCAPES**
*Mapping the Spiritual and Scientific Terrain*
*at the Dawn of the New Millenium*
MARK PARENT
An overview and analysis of nine of the most significant spiritual and
scientific movements of our time.
ISBN 1-896836-11-9

**PRAYER**
*The Hidden Fire*
TOM HARPUR
Brings the broad theological perspective of prayer to the personal level.
ISBN 1-896836-40-2

**SIN**
*A New Understanding of Virtue and Vice*
JAMES TAYLOR
Examines the fascinating origins and evolution of all seven deadly sins.
ISBN 1-896836-00-3

**RELIGIOUS ABUSE**
*A Pastor Explores the Many Ways*
*Religion Can Hurt As Well As Heal*
KEITH WRIGHT
This book addresses a difficult and controversial topic that occurs in every
denomination and at every level of the church.
ISBN 1-896836-47-X

**Find these titles at any fine bookstore, or call 1.800.663.2775 for
more information. Check our website www.joinhands.com**